TAKING RESPONSIBILITY

TAKING RESPONSIBILITY
PERSONAL LIABILITY UNDER ENVIRONMENTAL LAW

Stephen Tromans and Justine Thornton

Routledge
Taylor & Francis Group
LONDON AND NEW YORK

First published 2001 by Earthscan Publication Ltd.

2 Park Square, Milton Park, Abingdon, Oxon OX14 4RN
711 Third Avenue, New York, NY 10017, USA

Routledge is an imprint of the Taylor & Francis Group, an informa business

First issued in hardback 2017

A catalogue record for this book is available from the British Library

ISBN: 978-1-85383-597-1 (pbk)
ISBN: 978-1-138-45919-9 (hbk)

Cover design by Andrew Corbett

TABLE OF CONTENTS

LIST OF TABLES AND FIGURES

Tables

Figures

ABOUT THE AUTHORS

Stephen Tromans

Stephen Tromans MA (Cantab), Barrister, practices at 11 King's Bench Walk, specialising in environmental law and related areas. He is a Research Professor in Environmental Law at Nottingham Law School and the author of numerous books and other publications, including *The Environment Acts 1990–95*, *Planning Law, Practice and Precedents*, *Contaminated Land* and the *The Law of Nuclear Installations and Radioactive Substances*. He has advised the UK Parliamentary Committee on environmental issues and speaks widely on these topics in the UK and abroad.

Justine Thornton

Justine Thornton MA (Cantab), Barrister, is a member of the Environment Department at Simmons & Simmons, solicitors. She practised at the bar and worked in the Environment Department at the European Commission before joining Simmons & Simmons. She is co-author of *Environmental Law* (Sweet & Maxwell) and has published a number of articles on environmental issues in journals and newspapers. She lectures regularly on environmental law in Europe, the US and in the former Soviet states.

PREFACE

'A person who accepts the office of director of a particular company undertakes the responsibility of ensuring that he or she understands the nature of the duty a director is called upon to perform' (*Daniels* v *Anderson* [1995] 12 ACLC 614)

> **'STOP PRESS'**
>
> A new criminal offence of corporate killing has been proposed by the Government. The offence will cover deaths caused by 'management failure' in a company where its conduct has fallen far below what could reasonably be expected.
>
> Disasters like the sinking of the *Herald of Free Enterprise*, the King's Cross fire, the Clapham rail crash and the Southall rail crash prompted calls for changes in the law. None of the companies involved could be prosecuted for manslaughter despite the fact that inquiries found them to be at fault and meriting serious criticism.
>
> 23 May 2000

For companies operating in the 21st century environmental issues are a key element of good corporate governance. The environment may not seem to matter that much when set against the traditional 'big' corporate management issues. Companies are unlikely to be financially crippled by a typical fine for an environmental offence nor by damages from a single pollution incident. Looking at single events, however, misses the point: what is at issue is the cumulative effects of a policy of environmental responsibility or a lack of it. Today, there are too many environmental banana skins around for comfort. Slipping on one can be costly in several ways – in terms of direct liabilities, corporate image and morale, loss of confidence by regulators and actual or potential business partners, and in management time and effort.

What is true for a company is also true for its directors. Making directors personally liable for the actions of their companies is increasingly regarded as one of the most effective ways of protecting the environment. In addition, the standard of care and skill expected from directors is increasing. It is no longer enough for a director to rely on what he already knows. He must make sure he understands the role he is being asked to perform and perform, to an appropriate standard. He will not be able to pass his personal responsibility on to fellow directors, management and staff to the extent that he may have done in the past.

ACRONYMS AND ABBREVIATIONS

AC	Appeal Cases Report
BIL	Bata Industries Limited
BSO	Bata Shoe Organisation
EMS	environmental management system
ENDS	Environmental Data Services Report
Env LR	Environmental Law Reports
EPA	Environmental Protection Act 1986 (Canada)
All ER	All England Reports
HSE	Health and Safety Executive
IPC	integrated pollution control
IPPC	integrated pollution prevention and control
OWRA	Ontario Water Resources Act
QB	Queen's Bench

CHAPTER 1
PERSONAL LIABILITY: A GROWING RISK

Few people, when they become company directors, will spend a lot of time worrying about whether or not their appointment could result in having to face a criminal charge. We all know of the well publicised cases where directors and other officers have been accused of fraud, false accounting, insider dealing and the like. Less obvious is the risk of personal liability under environmental legislation, but these risks may well affect the honest director as well as the crook.

Consider the following extract from *The Times*.

'Pollution Danger for Owner Managers'

> *'Owner managers of small businesses will face an increased risk of fines and even prison this year if they breach the growing list of environmental regulations. In 1998 a man was jailed while five others and a company were ordered to pay fines and costs totalling £98,000 for asbestos waste offences. Roger Adams, head of the technical research department of the Association of Chartered Certified Accountants says: 'These days, company directors can go to prison for a wide range of environmental offences'* (*The Times*, 19.01.99).

The threat of personal liability is seen increasingly as one of the most effective ways of improving corporate responsibility under legislation for the protection of the environment. This is not a new idea:

> *'I think it would be a very good thing, instead of having fines as the punishment for breach of the law, to make it imprisonment, and flogging and pillory; I have no doubt that would keep them to it.* (Mr Richard Oastler, addressing a select committee at the House of Commons on early factory safety legislation, 1831).

In its enforcement policy (published in November 1999) the Environment Agency has stated that it will 'identify individuals, including company directors and managers, if it considers that a conviction is warranted and can be secured'.

Surveys indicate that the majority of the public and business executives favour holding individuals liable for environmental offences. Yet, personal liability remains very much the exception rather than the rule in the UK. The position is very different in some other jurisdictions, particularly the US and Canada, where executives are regularly prosecuted for environmental offences committed by their companies; in some cases, they receive prison sentences. The body of this report sets out the position in England and Wales (not Scotland) although details of an important Canadian case are set out in the Appendix.

What is certain is that the risk of this type of liability for UK company directors is increasing. The regulators and the public are becoming less tolerant of environmental non-compliance, and it is certainly true that incidents that would have been considered acceptable a few years ago are now resulting in prosecutions. This is reflected in the levels of fines imposed for offences. Although the fines have in the past been generally very low, they are now increasing. Although the examples given below relate to companies, the effect of the trend is likely to be felt by individuals who will be prosecuted.

EXAMPLE

In January 1999, the Port Authority responsible for the spill of oil from the *Sea Empress* was fined £4 million. This followed the spillage of 70,000 tonnes of oil in 1996 and a clean-up operation costing £100 million. The court said that the fine would have been much larger if a wealthier organisation had been found liable.

EXAMPLE

In 1990, Shell was fined £1 million for a major spillage of crude oil into the Mersey Estuary at Stanlow.

EXAMPLE

In March 1998, ICI was fined £300,000 for a major chloroform spill at its Runcorn works in Cheshire. Ed Gallagher, the Environment Agency's chief executive, commented that: 'In the past, fines for pollution have represented little more than loose change to big companies. I hope the scale of today's fine is an indication that the courts are beginning to understand the impact of what industry does when it pollutes the environment.'

Both the Government and the Environment Agency have for some time been encouraging the courts to impose larger fines for damage to the environment. The courts have themselves accepted that the level of fines are too low and Magistrates' courts are increasingly referring to the Crown Court for sentencing cases that they consider sufficiently serious to merit a higher punishment than they can give. The Court of Appeal has given guidelines to ensure that fines in health and safety cases reflect the gravity of the offence.

All directors (and other company officers) should therefore be aware of the law on personal liability for environmental offences, and how they can take steps to minimise the risks to themselves or their fellow directors of finding themselves before the criminal courts.

The following chapters explain the law governing personal liability, highlight areas of risk, and suggest some simple steps to reduce those risks.

CHAPTER 2
GENERAL PRINCIPLES

While the following chapters are mainly concerned with the personal liability of directors and other corporate officers, this chapter outlines the underlying principles of corporate and individual liability that it is important to be aware of.

Criminal and Civil Liability

There is a fundamental distinction between criminal and civil liability and as shown in Table 2.1 there are many important distinctions between them.

Crimes are generally acts that have a harmful effect on the public or the environment and do more than interfere with the private rights of individuals: punishment is a matter of public rather than private interest.

Civil liability results from the breach of some duty owed by one person to another. The duty may arise from a contract or from a duty in tort (for example, to take reasonable care or to avoid acts that unreasonably interfere with the enjoyment of land).

Environmental Crimes

Many breaches of environmental law are treated as crimes. The aim is to make clear to polluters society's moral condemnation of environmentally harmful activities. The main environmental crimes are listed in Table 2.2.

Civil Liability

Civil liability in the environmental context may arise in the following circumstances:

- death or personal injury caused by an explosion at an industrial site;
- disease caused by exposure to a hazardous substance such as asbestos;
- physical damage to property, for example, by an explosion caused by an accumulation of landfill gas;
- physical damage to crops caused by atmospheric pollution; and
- interference with the normal reasonable enjoyment of land caused by smells, dust, noise or vibrations.

Table 2.1 *Main Features of Legal Liability*

	Criminal	*Civil*
Procedure	Criminal Court: Magistrates or Crown Court	Civil Court: High Court or County Court
Proof	Onus on prosecution to prove crime to standard of 'beyond reasonable doubt', (no room for doubt).	Onus on plaintiff to establish liability on 'balance of probabilities' (more likely than not).
Prosecutor/Plaintiff	In general, any individual can bring a prosecution, although in practice most are brought by the UK's Crown Prosecution Service or regulatory bodies such as the Environment Agency or the Health and Safety Executive.	Only the person injured by the civil wrong can bring a civil action.
Sanction	Personal sanctions; the punishment is not related directly to the damage caused by the offence or to any need for compensation.	Damages are directly related to the consequences of the wrong. Punishment is not the objective.

Table 2.2 *Main Environmental Crimes*

Integrated pollution control (IPC) Integrated pollution prevention and control (IPPC)	• operating certain processes without an authorisation (permit) • breaching the conditions of an authorisation (permit) • failing to comply with an enforcement or prohibition notice
Waste	• treating, keeping, disposing of or depositing waste without a waste management licence • breaching the conditions of a waste management licence • failing to comply with the requirements of the duty of care
Water	• causing or knowingly permitting any poisonous, noxious or polluting matter to enter controlled waters • contravening the conditions of a discharge consent
Contaminated land (forthcoming)	• failing to comply with the requirements to clean up land specified in a remediation notice
Nuisance	• failing to comply with the requirements to abate nuisance caused by noise, dust, odour, smoke and animals, etc

Corporate Personality

A business may be conducted in one of three ways:

1 As a sole trader

2 As a partnership

3 As a company

A sole trader will be personally responsible for his own acts, both in criminal and in civil law.

> *EXAMPLE*
>
> Mr Swine runs a small butchers shop as a sole proprietor. As a result of appalling food hygiene conditions, a number of his customers contract food poisoning. He may be prosecuted and may also be liable to the customers.

Similarly, the members of a partnership will also be personally liable for those acts within the ordinary course of the partnership business.

> *EXAMPLE*
>
> Belt, Braces & Co is a firm of West End solicitors. The air conditioning plant at their offices is not properly maintained and causes an outbreak of legionnaires' disease. Personal, criminal and civil liability for each of the partners may follow.

These examples contrast with a business run through the medium of a company, whether a private limited company, public limited company, or company limited by guarantee.

From the date of its incorporation, a company is a separate legal body, distinct from its officers or shareholders. This is so even if the company is effectively a one-man business or a wholly-owned subsidiary. In general, apart from some exceptional circumstances relating to fraudulent or dishonest behaviour where the court may 'pierce the corporate veil', courts will not seek to go behind the facade to look at the actual control of a company.

> *EXAMPLE*
>
> Mr Swine, from the example above, decides to operate his butchers shop through a company, Trotters Limited. His personal liability will now be reduced as in general it is likely to be the company rather than he who will be prosecuted or sued.

Corporate Liability: Can a Company Commit an Environmental Crime?

In the early stages of the development of the law on companies, there were some doubts as to whether a company could be convicted of a criminal offence at all. After all, a company is a legal rather than a physical entity. It is now well accepted, however, that a company can be guilty of most offences and that while a company cannot physically be punished by imprisonment, it may be convicted and fined.

Many environmental crimes are of a 'strict liability' nature. In other words, the offence is caused by a certain act or physical circumstances, regardless of whether there was any intention to inflict harm or to cause the results that occurred. In these circumstances, finding the company liable is relatively straightforward.

> *EXAMPLE*
>
> A company was convicted of the offence of causing polluting matter to enter controlled waters. The tank holding process water overflowed because of a blocked pump. It was no excuse that the company had taken precautions to avoid such blockages. The fact was that the company had caused the incident. (*Alphacell* v *Woodward* [1972] AC 824.)

Many criminal offences, however, involve both a mental and physical element. There must be an act, coupled with the requisite knowledge, intention or other relevant state of mind. While a company can only know things or intend to undertake actions through its officers or agents, it is clear that the knowledge or intention of its officers and agents may be influential on the company.

> *EXAMPLE*
>
> A company was held liable for conspiracy to defraud by charging for a greater quantity of goods than actually delivered. The intention of the directors to defraud was influential on the company. (*R* v *ICR Haulage Ltd* [1947] 1 All ER 691.)

The issue is therefore the extent to which the actions and intentions of the 'officers and agents' may be attributed to the company.

The Company's 'Mind' and 'Hands'

A well-known analogy equates the company to a human body:

'It has a brain and nerve centre that controls what it does'	**ie**	Some people within the company are directors and managers who represent the directing mind and will of the company. The state of mind of these people is the state of mind of the company.
'It also has hands that hold the tools and act in accordance with directions from the centre'	**ie**	Some people are mere servants or agents who do nothing more than carry out the work and cannot be said to represent the company's mind or will.

(See *H L Bolton (Engineering) Co Ltd* v *T J Graham & Sons Ltd* [1957] 1 QB 159 (Lord Denning))

It is not particularly clear to what extent someone who is not at the top of the company's management can make the company criminally liable.

Someone who is in a position of managerial responsibility will not necessarily be regarded as part of the company's mind or will. It depends on how senior they are in the company's hierarchy.

> *EXAMPLE*
>
> The manager of a supermarket in a large chain was not to be identified with the mind or will of the company: he was only one of several hundred such managers (*Tesco Supermarkets Ltd* v *Nattrass* [1972] 1 AC 153).

Employees and Independent Contractors

The law draws an important distinction between employees and independent contractors.

Employees

The issue of when a company can be held criminally liable for the acts or omissions of its employees is a very important one as it is almost inevitably the actions of an employee that lead to a pollution incident. In an English case on shipping, the court felt that just because an offence is one of strict liability a company was not automatically responsible for the actions of its employees. Such responsibility would only arise if that clearly appeared to be the intention of the Parliament. Thus, where the offence was one of 'failing to take all reasonable steps', the court was of the view that Parliament would not have intended to impose criminal liability on a ship owner in the case of an omission by one of its employees, however junior in rank.

Regulatory authorities in the environmental field often seem to assume that a company will be vicariously liable for all the acts of its employees, provided they are acting within the scope of their employment. However, each offence must be looked at on its own merits.

In relation to civil law a company will generally be liable for the act of its employees provided that they are acting within the proper course of their employment.

In circumstances where the company might be criminally liable for the acts of its employees it is always important to check whether that employee was on a 'remit of his own'.

EXAMPLE

The employee of a waste company, Wastenutts Ltd, while unloading waste, acts contrary to standing instructions. Despite not following instructions, he will generally still be acting within the course of his employment, except perhaps in the most extreme of cases.

EXAMPLE

The employee of a waste company, Wantnot Ltd, secretly visited the company landfill site outside hours for unauthorised waste disposal. He will almost certainly be acting outside the course of his employment.

EXAMPLE

Two employees of a chemical company, ChemCom, while engaging in horseplay at work, damage a valve that causes the release of pollution in to a stream. It is unlikely that they can be said to be acting in the course of their employment.

Independent contractors

By contrast with employees, a company will generally not be vicariously liable for the acts of independent contractors. However, this principle needs to be treated with caution, as there have been cases where companies have been liable in such circumstances.

EXAMPLE

Yorkshire Water Company made use of sub-contractors to undertake maintenance work, on their behalf, on the local sewage system. The poor work of the sub-contractors resulted in sewage reaching a shallow lagoon on a popular holiday beach on a sunny August bank holiday. The provisions of the relevant statute hold the sewerage undertaker liable for discharges from its sewers even where the company itself has not caused the discharge. Here, the Water Company pleaded guilty and the judge commented that the company had the choice of supervising its contractors properly or else accepting the blame when things went wrong (*National Rivers Authority* v *Yorkshire Water Company* [1995] 1AC 444).

EXAMPLE

Abacus Co Ltd are forced to accept responsibility for the loud noise caused by its contractor. The court tells Abacus that it had a contract with its contractors and it could have used its powers under the contract to restrain the noise.

Applying These Principles

In each case it will be necessary to consider the components of the crime or civil action in question. If the incident was caused by a human act, was the person who carried out the act, someone for whom the company can be held responsible? Is any mental element required as well as the physical element? If so, does someone within the company, whose state of mind can be influential on the company, have the relevant intention?

EXAMPLE

A company owns an effluent storage tank. This develops a leak, resulting in pollutants entering a nearby river. No direct human action is involved. The company can be liable for having caused polluting matter to enter controlled waters because the offence is a 'strict liability' offence. (See *Alphacell* v *Woodward* above.)

EXAMPLE

An employee of AutoCorp, in the course of filling an oil storage tank, allows it to overflow, polluting a river. Again, the company can be liable for the offence of causing polluting matter to enter controlled waters. The employee is the 'hands' of the company and no intention to pollute is necessary.

EXAMPLE

A company provides false and misleading information to the Environment Agency in the course of applying for a waste management licence. The offence requires that the information was supplied 'knowing' it to be false. The question is whether a director, or someone else sufficiently senior to be regarded as the company's 'mind' or 'will', knew it was false.

It is important to note, however, that the courts may be moving away from this approach and taking a less tolerant view of companies' behaviour.

EXAMPLE

The site supervisor of a company decided to discharge a load of waste into a bin. He did not complete an advice note, as required by the licence. The supervisor was subsequently disciplined by the company. The company was charged with 'knowingly causing' waste to be deposited in breach of its licence. The company argued it could not be guilty as its senior management had not known about the breach of the licence. The court decided that it was sufficient that the senior management knew waste was being deposited on site. It was unnecessary to show more specific knowledge regarding particular loads on the part of the senior management (*Shanks Ltd* v *Environmental Agency* [1997] 2ALL ER 340)

CHAPTER 3
CRIMINAL LIABILITY OF DIRECTORS: GENERAL PRINCIPLES

Personal Liability

Other than in the smallest companies it will be rare for a director to be doing work that will result in his or her directly committing an offence. However, if he or she does so, there is no reason why a prosecution cannot follow. The following extract gives details of the first prosecution of a director in relation to integrated pollution control (IPC) regulations.

> *'The director of a Yorkshire drum cleaning company has been convicted of five breaches of an Integrated Pollution Control ('IPC') authorisation – becoming the first individual to be prosecuted for an IPC offence. The company operated a drum incinerator in Bradford, which came under IPC in 1994. The director was in charge of the site, which employed some 20 people.*
>
> *For many years, the operation attracted public complaints of black smoke and fumes. The Agency carried out a four-yearly review of the site's IPC authorisation in January 1997 that confirmed numerous authorisation breaches. Many of the breaches could have been prevented with little or no capital investment. It also became clear to the Environment Agency that the company was not prepared to upgrade the process by mid-1997, as required by its authorisation.*
>
> *The director was ordered to do 60 hours' of community service. The court accepted that he had no assets and that neither a fine nor a custodial sentence was appropriate'* (ENDS Report 281, June 1998, p50).

EXAMPLE

The director of a company poured a chemical down a drain. He thought it went into the sewer, but in fact the drain led straight into a watercourse and pollution resulted. He was prosecuted for water pollution offences.

Environmental offences relate not only to pollution. There are a number of ancillary offences which deal, for example, with matters like supplying false information in the course of making applications for authorisations or consents, or obstructing a pollution inspector. A director's actions may involve him or her in liability for such offences.

EXAMPLE

'Company director fined for assault on inspector'

A property developer was found guilty of assaulting a Health and Safety Executive (HSE) Inspector. The director pushed an inspector who had just served him with a prohibition notice, causing him to collide with a colleague who fell down a flight of stairs and injured his knees. (The *Safety and Health Practitioner*, August 1999)

It is also possible for a director who is the controlling mind or will of a company to take decisions that commit the company to a criminal course of action: effectively he commits an offence through the company that he controls. Whether the director is guilty of an offence will require careful consideration of the words of the relevant act, but liability is certainly a possibility.

EXAMPLE

Arthur and Bert decide that they are going to run a business of removing waste tyres from garages and factories and dumping them in an isolated field, thereby avoiding the need to have a waste site licence or to register as waste carriers (as well as for VAT and other inconveniences). They acquire a £100 company through which the enterprise will be run. Arthur and Bert could almost certainly be found liable for various offences including depositing waste without a licence.

EXAMPLE

Charles and Douglas are chairman and chief executive of a large and reputable waste company that runs a major landfill site. Their site licence is subject to a maximum tonnage of waste to be deposited each year. They are offered a very lucrative contract that they know will involve taking more waste than the licence conditions permit. They sign the contract, hoping that the waste authority will not pick up on the breach of condition. Charles and Douglas could be liable for the breaches of the company.

Statutory Liability

All of the examples given above arise essentially from the director's own acts or decisions. However, beyond this straightforward category of personal liability, there is another kind of liability that does not depend on personal actions and which applies only to directors and similar officers of companies. This stems from provisions in a number of Acts of Parliament which state that where a company is guilty of an offence, a director or similar officer of the company may also be guilty in certain circumstances.

The provisions are based on the idea that a director must accept some degree of responsibility for the actions of his company. It has been common form for many years to include in environmental and health and safety legislation, a section along the following lines:

> *'Where an offence committed by a body corporate is proved to have been committed with the consent or connivance of, or to be attributable to any neglect on the part of any director, manager, secretary or similar officer of the body corporate or any person who was purporting to act in any such capacity, he as well as the body corporate shall be guilty of that offence and shall be liable to be proceeded against and punished accordingly.'*

The area of law and Act of Parliament where a provision on director's liability is given in Table 3.1.

Table 3.1 *Statutory Provisions for Director's Liability*

Area of law	*Act*	*Section*
Environmental Protection	Control of Pollution Act 1974	87
Environmental Protection	Environmental Protection Act 1990	157
Water Pollution	Water Resources Act 1991	217
Trade Effluent	Water Industry Act 1991	210
Radioactive Substances	Radioactive Substances Act 1993	36
Health and Safety	Health and Safety at Work (etc) Act 1974	37

The provisions may be represented in a flow chart (see Figure 3.1).

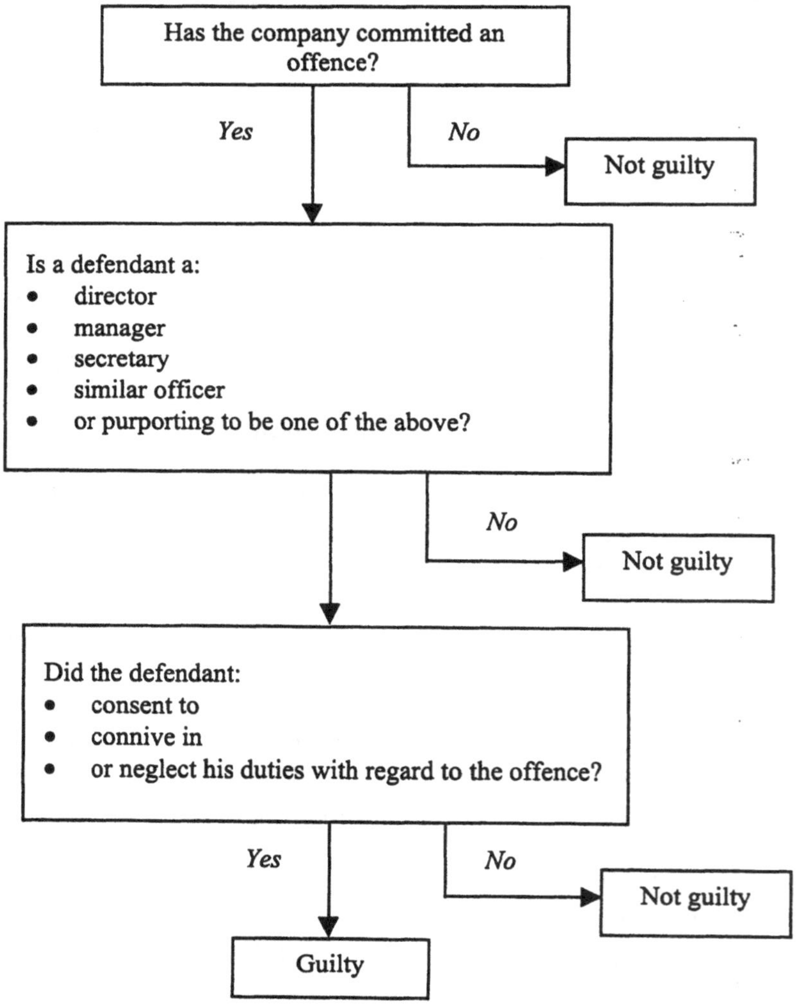

Figure 3.1 *The Structure of Director's Liability*

So for all of the offences under these acts (and others) a director, secretary, manager or similar officer of a company can be liable in the circumstances set out above. It is therefore extremely important to understand what the section means in practice. The rest of this chapter considers the issue of *who* can be liable while the next chapter considers the *circumstances* in which they can be liable. The position of non-executive directors, shareholders and other advisors is considered in Chapter 5.

Directors

Section 741(1) of the Companies Act 1985 defines a director as 'any person occupying the position of director, by whatever name called'.

There will generally be no doubt as to who the directors of a company are. Their particulars must be filed at Companies House and can be discovered from the register of companies. The company's memorandum and articles will deal with their appointment, resignation and removal. Someone may have the job title of 'director' (for example, technical director, regional sales directors) but will *not* be a director in the legal sense.

Secretary

This does not of course mean a secretary in the usual administrative sense: the company secretary is a legal officer of the company whose identity will be clearly known. He/she, like the director, will have his/her particulars filed with Companies House.

Manager

Like 'secretary', this does not mean a manager in the everyday sense of the word: it means someone who genuinely manages the affairs of the company and is to that extent in a position of control of the company as a whole. Many people may be called 'manager' in the sense of having responsibility and some degree of authority over part of the company's undertaking - for example, a store manager, site manager, office manager, regional sales manager, etc. This, of itself, will not make them a manager in the sense of managing the company's affairs. Whether they are a manager in the strict sense may depend on factors such as the size and structure of the company. The following examples from decided cases may help to illustrate this.

EXAMPLE

Mr Boal was the assistant general manager of Foyles Bookshop in Charing Cross Road. His primary duty was chief buyer and he had no training in managerial or health and safety matters. He was placed in charge of the shop while the general manager was away on holiday. Unfortunately for him, an inspection of the shop premises by the local fire authority revealed serious breaches of the fire certificate. Mr Boal was charged under the Fire Precautions Act 1971 on the basis that he was a 'manager'. He pleaded guilty and was given a suspended prison sentence. On appeal, the Court suggested that there was some doubt as to whether he was a 'manager' within the terms of the legislation. Although Mr Boal was fourth in the hierarchy of the company below Mrs Foyle, (the managing director), her husband and Mr Cruikshank, the general manager, the Court held that Mr Boal was not a 'manager' for the purposes of the provision in the statute. (*R* v *Boal* [1992] 3 All ER 177)

EXAMPLE

While painting the Albert Bridge in Glasgow, an employee of Strathclyde Regional Council fell to his death in the Clyde. The Council's Director of Roads was charged with offences under the Health and Safety at Work (etc) Act. It was held that the Director was sufficiently senior and powerful to fall within the class of 'director, manager or similar officer'. He had general responsibility for implementing the Council's policy on health and safety (*Armour* v *Skeen* [1976] SLT 71).

EXAMPLE

The manager of a supermarket, as one of several hundred such managers within the company, could not be equated with the company in the sense of having real control over the company (*Tesco Supermarkets Ltd* v *Nattrass* [1972] AC 153).

Similar Officers

The words 'or similar officer' are of the nature of a sweep-up clause, but on general legal principles must be read in the light of the previous words 'director, manager or secretary' and therefore do not widen significantly the class of people who are potentially liable. Clearly, it could cover someone such as the chief executive of a company should he/she not fall within any of the other categories.

Defectively Appointed Officers

It is not unknown for directors or company secretaries to be defectively appointed. This situation is caught by the words 'or . . . purporting to act in such capacity'.

EXAMPLE

Linda is supposedly a director of LindaCoi Ltd, being named on the notepaper as such and describing herself and acting as such. However, by mistake the correct procedures were not followed so she has not been duly appointed. Nonetheless, she is purporting to act as a director and can be held liable as such.

CHAPTER 4
CONSENT, CONNIVANCE AND NEGLECT

As pointed out in the previous chapter, being a director or similar officer is not of itself enough to make someone liable where the company commits an offence. The usual statutory provision also requires one of three things. That the offence has been:

- committed with his or her consent;

  or
- committed with his or her connivance;

  or
- attributable to any neglect on his or her part

Each of these issues need to be considered in turn.

Consent

According to the classic definition, consent involves some affirmative act or approval.

> *'It would seem that where a director consents to the commission of an offence by his company, he is well aware of what is going on and agrees to it'* (*Huckerby* v *Elliott* [1970] 1 All ER 189, at page 194).

In other words there must be:

- knowledge; and
- positive approval

EXAMPLE

Felix, a director, is told by one of his line managers that there is a problem with pollution control equipment and that releases are occurring in excess of the plant's permitted levels. The only way to stop the releases is to shut the plant down for investigation and repair the equipment. Felix has production targets to meet and gives an order to his manager not to shut down the line. Felix has consented to the breach of licence.

EXAMPLE

Donald is company secretary of Ordure Limited, a small waste company. He knows that the site licence conditions at one of the company's landfill sites are not being complied with, but refuses to sanction the expenditure that would be required to rectify the problems. Donald has therefore consented to the breach of licence conditions.

Connivance

'Connivance' is a legal term that was used a great deal in the old law of divorce in the context of a partner's adultery, and many of the cases involving the term arise in a matrimonial setting.

The word implies acquiescence in circumstances or conduct that is reasonably likely to lead to an offence being committed. Positive knowledge of the offence is not necessary, but something more than ignorance, inattention or negligence is required. The idea is summed up best in the following extract from a leading textbook on criminal law: '...knowledge (including wilful blindness) plus negligent failure to prevent'.

Another way of putting it is the following extract from a decided case:

> *'Where he [the director] connives at the offence committed by the company he is equally well aware of what is going on but his agreement is tacit, not actively encouraging what happens but letting it continue and saying nothing about it.'* (*Huckerby* v Elliott [1970] 1 All ER 189, at page 194)

EXAMPLE

Director Clive suspects that workers in the paint shop of his plant are taking short cuts in some of their practices, which breach health and safety and environmental legislation. However, he takes no action, effectively 'turning a blind eye'.

EXAMPLE

Director Simon leaves the arrangement of waste disposal to one of his supervisors. He is aware that waste is taken for disposal at a landfill site run by Ordure Limited. He begins to hear disturbing reports about how the site is operated from drivers who deliver waste there. However, he takes the view that 'waste disposal isn't a matter for a director' and does not raise the issue with the supervisor or seek any further information. He has connived in the breach of duty of care requirements.

Neglect

Neglect is wider than 'consent' or 'connivance'. It has been said to imply:

> *'... failure to perform a duty which the person knows or ought to know'* (*Re Hughes* [1943] 2 All ER 269).

However, the duties of directors are not absolute and the question is: what is the true extent of the duty of the director or officer in question?

Matters to be considered in ascertaining a director's or officer's duty include:

- the nature of the company's business;
- the manner in which the company's work is distributed between directors and other officials; and
  - whether or not it is that manner of distribution reasonable in the circumstances;
  - whether it is consistent with the company's written constitution in its articles of association.

It is clear that not all directors of a company will be under the same duties. For instance, one director may have specific responsibility for matters of health and safety and environmental protection. His duties will be more onerous for his particular area.

> *EXAMPLE*
>
> In the Scottish case, *Armour* v *Skeen* ([1995] SLT 71) to which reference was made in Chapter 3, the Director of Roads of Strathclyde Regional Council was found guilty under health and safety legislation following an employee's death. The Council had adopted a general safety policy and the director was responsible for issuing a detailed safety policy and operational instructions to implement it. He had failed in that duty.

Expertise

The standards expected from directors are increasing. In the old days a director was not expected to have any special skill beyond the job skills he possessed and directors were entitled to rely upon fellow directors or staff unless there was a reason to question them.

However, the duties are undoubtedly more onerous now. The courts have added an objective test to a director's performance;

> *'it is the conduct of a reasonably diligent person having both – the general knowledge, skill and experience that may reasonably be expected of a person carrying out the same functions as are carried out by that director in relation to the company and by the general knowledge and skill and experience that that director has'* (*Re D'Jan* v *London Limited* [1994] 1BCLC561 Hoffman L J).

Delegation

The more onerous standards have in turn reduced the extent to which a director can rely on his fellow directors and staff.

The ability to rely on the delegation of a director's duties is also subject to qualification by what can be called the 'Three S principle':

- suspicion;
- supervision; and
- support.

A director cannot ignore matters that give him/her grounds for *suspicion*. If he/she is aware that those with delegated responsibility for environmental matters do not have the right attitude, he/she will need to take action to correct it.

> *EXAMPLE*
>
> Barbara, a director, reports to the board on environmental matters. She delegates operational matters to manager Bertha. It becomes increasingly apparent that Bertha is not taking her duties seriously, that practices are lax, and that proper records and paperwork in relation to waste disposal are not being kept. Due to pressure of work in other areas, Barbara sweeps her growing concerns 'under the carpet'.

A director must adequately *supervise* those to whom he/she delegates.

EXAMPLE

Director Charles has responsibility for environment and safety across the company's six plants. In each plant he has a manager responsible for environment and safety, but he never visits them and asks for a cursory written report only once a year to put in the company's annual 'environmental review'.

A director must ensure that those to whom he/she delegates are given proper *support* in terms of resources and training.

EXAMPLE

Director Deirdre is nominated by the board of her company to implement the company's environmental policy, which includes compliance with all applicable laws. She delegates this task to Frank, a middle manager with no environmental training and an inadequate budget. Frank is overloaded with numerous other tasks, including the organisation of the company's centenary celebrations, and consequently cannot cope with environmental compliance.

CHAPTER 5
NON-EXECUTIVE DIRECTORS, SHAREHOLDERS AND OTHERS

Non-executive Directors

Many companies have a number of independent non-executive directors on their books. More than 95 per cent of the top 300 UK companies now have non-executive directors.

It has been claimed that the ways in which a non-executive director can contribute to a company include:

- the provision of impartial and considered advice in relation to the evolution of company strategy by the board;
- the strengthening of the leadership qualities of the board;
- the striking of a correct balance between the interests of the various persons with a stake in the financial health of the company, for example, shareholders, employees, directors and creditors;
- monitoring the performance of the board as a whole, and reporting to shareholders if its performance or attitudes are seen as unsatisfactory;
- achieving high standards of financial probity, probably through serving on the company's audit committee;
- enhancing the company's credibility with investors; and
- widening the company's range of useful contacts.

The appointment of non-executive directors has been urged by a number of influential bodies such as the Institutional Shareholders' Committee, the London Stock Exchange and the Institute of Directors.

Position of Non-executive Directors

English law does not recognise any distinct office of non-executive director and accordingly in principle, the duties and obligations of a non-executive director are the same as those of an executive director: he/she is not allowed any dispensation merely because he/she is not involved in the routine management of the company.

However, as mentioned earlier, the law recognises that not all directors perform the same duties. It would not be reasonable to attribute to a non-executive director the sort of detailed knowledge of the company's business that would be possessed by an executive director.

In theory, therefore, a non-executive director may be potentially liable in the same way as an executive director where environmental offences were committed with his/her consent, connivance or neglect. For this reason it is vital that serving and intending non-executive directors should be aware of the circumstances in which such liability may arise.

In practice, much will depend upon the duties that the non-executive director undertakes. Provided he performs those duties to a reasonable standard, that it is reasonable for him to confine or curtail his activities in that way, and that he does not culpably close his eyes to malpractice of which he should reasonably take notice, the non-executive director probably runs little risk of personal liability.

In particular, it is perhaps unlikely that a non-executive director will have specific operational responsibilities relating to environmental matters. However, as good environmental management and standards play a greater role in corporate governance, so non-executive directors may become increasingly involved in this sphere, in a supervisory or advisory role.

EXAMPLE

Ambridge Manufacturing Corporation is convicted of a number of pollution and waste-related offences. The unsatisfactory position that led to those offences was known to the board of directors, but not to Lord Borchester, a non-executive director. Lord Borchester's main role is to chair the company's audit and remuneration committees and as a retired merchant banker he has no specialist expertise in environmental issues. It is unlikely that he would be guilty of any offence.

EXAMPLE

Carter's Packaging Ltd is convicted of a number of pollution and waste-related offences. Miss Dudley is a well-known ecologist who was appointed as a non-executive director specifically to advise the company on its environmental responsibilities and performance. Despite being aware from her various site inspections of the circumstances that led to the offences she failed to draw the serious implications to the attention of the board. Directors say that had they known of her real concerns they would have acted to resolve the problems. Miss Dudley is probably vulnerable in those circumstances.

A newly appointed non-executive director appointed for their environmental expertise should take the following steps:

- Make sure it is clear why he/she has been appointed and ensure this is properly recorded.
- Familiarise him/herself with the relevant aspects of the company's business.
- Satisfy him/herself that the professionals responsible for environmental issues in the company's business are competent to do the tasks that they are set.
- He/she should not assume that their duties are limited to intermittent attendance at board meetings. A non-executive director is increasingly expected to take a more pro-active role.
- If a decision is required about the environmental management of the company he/she should be satisfied that the decision they take is made on the basis of his skill and is the decision that would be expected of someone appointed specifically for their environmental expertise.

Shareholders

Several Acts of Parliament concerned with the environment and health and safety contain the following provision:

> *'where the affairs of a body corporate are managed by its members, subsection (1) above [dealing with directors, secretaries and similar officers] shall apply in relation to the acts or defaults of a member in connection with his functions of management as if he were a director of the body corporate'.*

This provision is contained in section 157(2) of the Environmental Protection Act 1990 and in the corresponding sections of the Health and Safety at Work (etc) Act 1974, the Water Resources Act 1991, and other environmental legislation.

In simple terms, the provision that:

- where a company's affairs are managed by a shareholder or shareholders, then
- those shareholders are treated as directors, in that
- if they consented to, connived in, or by their neglect, caused the company to commit an offence, then
- they can be prosecuted personally.

EXAMPLE

Ambroses is a family business founded by Barry and his wife Carrie. Barry and Carrie retire as directors, leaving sons Damion and Eammon to assume the directorships. However, Barry and Carrie retain their controlling shareholding and exert pressure on Damion and Eammon as to how the business is run on a day-to-day basis. They override Damion and Eammon's wishes to invest in new equipment necessary to comply with environmental law, on the basis that it is 'new fangled nonsense, and not how we got where we are today'.

Barry and Carrie may be liable because they are managing the company's affairs. Damion and Eammon could also be liable in their capacity as actual directors.

A 'normal' shareholder who simply holds shares and exercises his/her normal shareholder's rights will not be vulnerable under this provision.

'Boards of Environmental Responsibility'

There is a trend among larger companies in some sectors to appoint external environmental advisory boards.These may be called 'environment panels', 'boards of environmental responsibility' or similar. Often they will be composed of the 'great and good' – members of the House of Lords, academics, environmental media figures, etc. They may be paid, or may simply have their expenses reimbursed.

Their function is usually to act as a sort of environmental barometer, to provide an external and objective check on how the company is performing environmentally. They will be provided with information by the company and will probably be taken on visits to the company's various sites. They will often produce an annual review for the company's directors, shareholders, customers, bankers etc. Doubtless, the company feels it gains an objective viewpoint and a measure of additional credibility with the outside world.

The actual legal responsibilities of such panels are a murky and complex area. Members of such panels will only be potentially liable if they are directors or similar officers or are purporting to act in such a capacity. It is most unlikely that any panel members would be directors, as this would defeat the very point of achieving objectivity. However, are they effectively assuming the responsibility of directors in relation to their sphere of competence? Much will depend on the detailed relationship between the panel and the board of directors and how influential the panel really is.

EXAMPLE

Baroness Weatherfield is a former minister in the Department of the Environment. She accepts an appointment by Big Brand to head its environmental responsibility panel, for which she is paid £25,000 a year. The board of the company depends very heavily on the advice of the panel and invariably complies with its recommendations. By oversight, the Baroness and her fellow panellists fail to detect and alert the board to serious and quite obvious breaches of environmental legislation. Baroness Weatherfield may be vulnerable.

CHAPTER 6
AN INSPECTOR CALLS

What happens when a pollution inspector arrives on site claiming that a serious pollution incident has occurred and asking to interview a representative of the company and/or any personnel on site. If there is no procedure in place to deal with this event then such incidents can be a source of major panic. It is important to be aware of:

- the inspector's powers;
- the implications of what is said to him or her; and
- the rights of anyone who is questioned.

Powers of Investigation

Pollution control legislation gives inspectors wide powers of investigation. The typical powers given to Environment Agency and local authority inspectors include the power to:

- enter premises and to do so with other authorised personnel and equipment;
- examine and investigate the site;
- direct that the site, or part of the site, be left undisturbed during the examination;
- take photographs, measurements and recordings;
- take samples;
- question personnel on site and require answers;
- require the production of records and documents;
- require the assistance of personnel on site;
- deal with substances believed to have caused, or to be likely to cause, pollution of the environment or harm to human health; and
- serve a notice requiring the production of information.

An inspector has a wide remit to carry out whatever examination and investigations he thinks are necessary in the circumstances. He can direct that the premises be left undisturbed for as long as is necessary to continue the examination or investigation and he can also take any necessary measurements, photographs or recordings. Information obtained as a result of exercising any of the above-mentioned powers is admissible in court as evidence against the company or any individual, even if the inspectors arrive on site without the company's consent. In most cases, failure to co-operate with the inspector, or obstructing the inspector, is an offence in its own right.

The Power of Entry

An inspector can enter a company's premises if he thinks it is reasonably necessary to do so. If he thinks he is likely to be refused entry he may obtain a warrant entitling him to enter the premises specified in the warrant. In an emergency where he thinks there is an immediate risk of serious pollution of the environment then his powers are even broader. He can enter premises at any time and by force if necessary.

The Power to Take Samples

As well as taking samples of any articles or substances that they find on the site, the inspector can dismantle and test the articles/substances and keep any they find, either to examine or to ensure that they are not tampered with before they have finished examining them and to ensure that they are available for use in any court case. If necessary they can destroy the articles/substances. Before doing so the inspector must follow certain procedures that include enquiring about the dangers of his proposed course of action. In addition the inspector can also take samples of air, water or land on site or in the vicinity, carry out experimental borings and set up any monitoring and other apparatus there.

The Power to Require Production of Records

Any records that a company is required to keep as a condition of any licence must be shown to an inspector if requested as must any other records that the inspector considers will help him carry out their investigation. It is not clear whether records include emails and correspondence as well as licences and other related documents. Emails/correspondence should not be shown until they are specifically requested and then the risk of revealing information contained in any correspondence must be balanced against the risk of antagonising the inspector. Any documents protected by legal professional privilege do not have to be shown. This includes any communications with in-house lawyers or external lawyers. It does not, however, cover communications with, or advice from, other professional advisers such as engineers or accountants.

The Power to Question, Interview and Request Information

The power to question, interview and request information is the most frequently exercised power and the one that raises the most problems. The following are the main types of questioning that may be encountered:

Informal questioning: An inspector may well ask questions while visiting the site or undertaking an investigation. There is no obligation to answer such questions.

Individuals have a right, under common law, to remain silent and a similar right against self-incrimination. However, in the interests of co-operation, site personnel usually try to be helpful. This may have benefits in terms of public image and future relations with the regulator, but be aware that it may also provide the evidence to prosecute, not only the company, but also individuals.

Although the general rule is that the answers given during informal discussions cannot be used as evidence in court, there is one important exception. A confession made by an accused person or on behalf of a company may be given in evidence against them or the company. The term 'confession' is widely defined and includes any statement wholly or partly adverse to the person who made it. This covers all confessions made to a person in authority whether or not made under caution.

Employees may make a confession or admission with regard to any offence they may have personally committed but it is unlikely that such an individual could make a confession or admission with regard to any offence that the company may have committed. This is because such an admission is not likely to be within that person's scope of authority to act on behalf of the company and would therefore not be an admission made by an accused person. However, it will depend upon the facts of the case and in particular upon the relevant individual and his authority and scope of employment, in relation to the matters being investigated.

However, a senior manager or director, in view of his position within the organisation, may reasonably be expected to have the authority to make an admission against the company's interests, (or where a director has been given express authority by the board of directors to speak on its behalf). It could also demonstrate consent, connivance or neglect by the individual.

EXAMPLE

Mr Harris from the Environment Agency arrives at Synthchem's premises to investigate a leak of toluene. Fred, one of the directors, apologises to Mr Harris and explains the company had not managed to carry out necessary repairs to a bund because of an urgent deadline for an order. The statement by Fred could be used by the Agency against the company in court and to show Fred had consented to the offence.

However, any admissions made in an informal discussion are rarely relied upon in court during a prosecution. In the main, this is due to the strict rules for interviewing under caution as discussed below.

Investigative questions: In addition to informal questioning, an officer has the power to require anyone he/she thinks may help the investigation to answer questions and to sign a declaration as to the truth of the answers. Anyone questioned in this way must answer. As a general rule the answers cannot be used in any subsequent proceedings. The power is available to the inspector to carry out a proper investigation rather than to trap anyone.

However, although the person answering the questions is protected from self-incrimination, that protection does not extend to anyone else. So if staff are required to answer questions and they implicate a senior manager then this would be admissible against the manager and the company unless the court comes to the view that the admission of the evidence would have such an adverse effect on the fairness of the proceedings that it ought not to admit it.

The protection from the evidence being used in a court hearing only applies to oral answers and not to any documents obtained (if they can be admitted into court under other rules).

Questions under caution: When an inspector considers that an offence may have been committed by a company, it might ask company staff to attend at its offices for an interview under caution. This will be a formal interview.

Any confession or admissions made during an interview under caution may be used in any subsequent criminal proceedings. Again, a confession must have been made by the person accused and can only be used as evidence against that person. If anything is said by senior management then this could be used against the company because they have the authority to speak on behalf of the company.

The fact that an interview is conducted under caution does not endow the answers given with any special evidential weight. Only those answers that amount to the confession or admissions of guilt are allowable as evidence in court. However, in practice much of an interview is allowed into court by agreement between the parties where there would be no prejudice to the defendant in the background information revealed during questioning being seen by the Magistrates or a jury.

The rights of interviewees

Anyone under investigation for a possible offence has certain rights; this is true whether the investigation is being carried out by the police or by a pollution inspector.

In particular, anyone questioned has the right to stay silent and refuse to answer questions. Whether it is sensible to exercise this right depends on the circumstances and in many companies there is an understandable wish to be seen to be co-operative, open and helpful with the regulators. It is not obligatory to attend an interview under caution. It is always possible to write to the Agency in advance of any proposed interview requesting to see in writing the questions that the Agency propose to put. A decision can then be made as to whether to attend the interview or to choose to give written responses.

EXAMPLE

The Environment Agency writes to Bunsen Limited saying that in its opinion an offence has been committed with the leak of chemicals in to nearby groundwater. It asks that the site manager and the employee who was working on site when the incident occurred attend the Agency's offices for an interview on caution. The manager replies to the Agency declining to attend for an interview but asking the Agency to send a list of questions and promising that the company will make every effort to give full, accurate and complete replies.

When investigating offences or charging offenders, a regulatory authority must follow a code of practice used by police created under the Police and Criminal Evidence Act 1984. The aim of the code is to ensure that anyone being questioned is not put under pressure or intimidated.

Any interview must be tape recorded, (unless it is clear from the outset that no prosecution will ensue) in order to ensure that there is an impartial and accurate record of the interview.

Before starting the interview the interviewee must be cautioned. The caution will take the following form:

> *'You do not have to say anything. But it may harm your defence if you do not mention when questioned something which you later rely on in court. Anything you do say may be given in evidence.'*

The caution is to remind the person being interviewed of his common law right to silence, that he is under no obligation to answer questions and is under no obligation to incriminate himself.

The inspector cautioning the interviewee must identify himself and state the offence he believes has been committed. The officer must ensure that the person being interviewed understands the caution. He must also ensure that the interviewee understands that he is not under arrest and is not obliged to remain at the interview.

Anyone being interviewed has the right to speak to a solicitor, by telephone if necessary, before answering any questions.

Where the investigating officer has acted reasonably and in accordance with the appropriate code of practice then any evidence obtained is likely to be admissible in court. However, where evidence has been obtained improperly or unfairly it may be deemed inadmissible on the basis that the admission of the evidence would have an adverse effect on the fairness of the proceedings of the court.

EXAMPLE

Mr Goodyear, a waste regulation officer from the south west region of the Environment Agency, spots a plume of grey-green smoke being emitted from a waste transfer station. He walks onto the premises without permission in order to get a better look and takes photographs of the smoke while there. In a later prosecution, the photographs are produced as evidence of the emissions of noxious substances from the transfer station. The court feels that the evidence, although obtained by trespassing, should be admissible given the circumstances of the case.

EXAMPLE

Douglas Marchant was interviewed voluntarily in his office by the Ministry of Environment in Toronto, Canada. He was cautioned and told by the Ministry of Environment Investigators that he need not give a statement but, if he did, anything that he said would be used against him. The investigator then read a provision of a Canadian Statute in which it was suggested that if he did not provide information he could be charged with obstruction of justice. Mr Marchant's statement was ruled inadmissible on the basis that the investigators had effectively compelled Mr Marchant to give a statement, which otherwise he had a legal right not to give if he so chose. (See Appendix I on the Canadian Case Study – The Bata Industries Case.)

The Inspector Arrives

Any inspector arriving on site should be asked for their authorisation to come on site and the scope of that authorisation. If they don't have the necessary authorisation, it may be possible to exclude any evidence produced in court, obtained as a result of the exercise of their powers. A note should be taken of any visits, including the name of the officer, the date of the visit, the reason for the visit and the company personnel who dealt with the matter. The officer should be asked for details of the authority's understanding of the alleged incident, including the date and time of the incident, the person who notified the Environment Agency and whether any damage is alleged to have been caused.

CHAPTER 7
WILL THEY PROSECUTE?

The decision whether or not to prosecute is always a matter of discretion for the relevant authority. Even if there is sufficient evidence for a successful prosecution, the regulator may feel that the public interest is best served by issuing a formal warning or infraction notice, rather than by prosecution.

If an offender is willing to accept his guilt then the regulator may decide to offer a 'formal caution' or a written warning as an acceptable alternative to prosecution. A warning may be in the form of a letter from the regulators stating that in its opinion the offender has committed an offence that will be taken into account in the event of any future problems. A formal caution is a statement in writing signed by the offender accepting that he committed an offence. A record is kept of the caution and may influence decisions by the regulator as to prosecution should the offender commit a similar offence in the future. If the offender is subsequently found guilty of a further offence, then any sentence may take into account the offence for which he was cautioned.

In deciding whether or not to prosecute the regulatory authority will look at all of the circumstances surrounding the offence. The matter may also be referred to internal lawyers. No regulatory authority would accept that it can bind itself in advance as to whether or not to prosecute in particular circumstances: a decision must be made in each case on its own facts. However, many authorities have issued internal or semi-public prosecution guidelines in an attempt to achieve a measure of consistency.

The Environment Agency has an enforcement and prosecution policy. It states that the Agency will consider the following factors in deciding whether or not to prosecute:

- The environmental effect of the offence. How serious were the consequences? Were fish killed or people affected? Was a nuisance caused?
- The foreseeability of the offence or the circumstances leading to it.
- The intent of the offender, individually and/or corporately.
- The accused's past record. Is this a 'one-off' incident or another chapter in a history of irresponsible conduct?
- The accused's attitude to the incident. Did the accused take steps to mitigate the consequences of the incident and co-operate with the regulatory authority in so doing? Have steps been taken to avoid any repetition of the incident?
- The deterrent effect of a prosecution on the offender and others.
- The personal circumstances of the offender.

The Agency will normally prosecute:

- where the environment has been significantly damaged;
- where operations are carried out without a licence;
- where the breaches of licences are persistent;
- where a site has failed to comply with a notice requiring action;
- where operators have acted in reckless disregard for management or quality standards; or
- where an operator has given false information to the Agency or refused to comply with a request for information or has obstructed the Agency in its duties.

As well as such obvious factors, it should be remembered that regulatory bodies may be under political pressure to prosecute, either because they are seen as not being sufficiently tough, or because certain types of offence are particularly 'high profile' or are seen as sufficiently serious. This may be particularly true of local authority officers, who are directly accountable to locally elected politicians.

It should also be remembered that it is open for private individuals or public interest groups to bring prosecutions. There have been examples of prosecutions, sometimes successful, by bodies such as Greenpeace and by angling associations. These prosecutions may be motivated by the desire for publicity, or to embarrass the 'polluter', or from a feeling that the regulatory bodies are not taking breaches of legislation (technical breaches in some cases) sufficiently seriously.

There is also the decision as to who should be prosecuted. In the vast majority of cases the prosecution will simply proceed against the company. In some cases, there may be a prosecution against the individual employee who caused the breach. The risk of such a prosecution may be increased if the employee's action extended beyond the scope of employment so that the acts were those of the employee's own making. The degree of personal culpability is also very relevant.

Finally, there is the decision as to whether proceedings should also be taken against a director, secretary or similar officer. Clearly, before proceeding in this way the prosecutor will wish to be satisfied that there is evidence of consent, connivance or neglect leading to the offence on the part of the relevant officer. Such proceedings are more likely in the case of small or medium-sized companies where directors are likely to be closely involved in day-to-day operational matters, or where the director's acts can be very closely identified with those of the company.

A decision to prosecute a director will obviously mean considerably more work for the prosecuting authority. It will also make the case 'high profile' and may make it more likely to be vigorously defended. It therefore seems likely that the power to prosecute a director will continue to be used sparingly and with discrimination, in cases where:

- there is a perceived high degree of personal culpability;
- the case is seen as particularly serious, and especially if death or serious injury has resulted;
- the company is seen as irresponsible and there is a wish to use 'shock tactics' to act as a future deterrent; or

- there is a wish to provide an example and clear deterrent for company officers generally or in a particularly problematic industry sector.

Stopping a Prosecution

Even if a regulatory authority decides to prosecute, it may change its mind and withdraw charges against a company or an individual. This can happen for various reasons including the discovery of new evidence and witnesses changing their version of events. The prosecution may be persuaded to accept a 'plea bargain'. If an accused is charged with a number of offences he/she agrees to plead guilty to some of the offences. In return, the prosecution may decide not to offer any evidence on the other charges which are then withdrawn from the court.

An accused may also apply to the court to have the prosecution discontinued on the basis of what is known as an 'abuse of process', namely either that it is unfair to try him, or he will not be able to receive a fair trial. There have been several recent examples of this in environmental prosecutions, where the court has found that the Environment Agency had, in effect, misled the companies concerned. This is, however, a rare step for a court to take as the courts are very reluctant to interfere with a decision to prosecute.

EXAMPLE

'Landmark IPC prosecution rocks Agency enforcement policy'

Petrus Oils refinery experienced a series of problems over odour. The Agency eventually brought 11 charges against the company. Petrus applied for one of the charges to be stayed claiming that the Agency had abused the legal process. The charge in question was that Petrus Oil had breached a condition of its IPC authorisation for its oil refinery by not having a flame failure device fitted in its chimney stack. Petrus Oil claimed that there had been such a device at the start of the plant's operations but due to odour problems, changes to the plant required by the Agency Inspector led to the system being deactivated. The court ordered the charge to be discontinued as it was 'manifestly unfair and oppressive' (*ENDS Report* 286: November 1998).

CHAPTER 8
THE CONSEQUENCES OF CONVICTION

What are the likely consequences for the director or officer convicted of an environmental offence? The obvious point to make is that the financial and other material consequences may be far less devastating than the personal stigma of having acquired a criminal record.

What factors will the court take into account in deciding on sentence? It is difficult to predict the outcome of a decision on sentencing. In other areas of law, the courts or the government issue guidance on sentencing decisions: there is, however, at present no guidance for environmental offences (although at the time of writing the Government is consulting on this). The effect is that courts have a lot of discretion. The Court of Appeal has recently given some guidance on sentencing for health and safety offences and much of this will be relevant for environmental offences.

In *R* v *Howe & Son (Engineers) Limited* [1999] 2 All ER 249, the court said it was appropriate to consider any mitigating and aggravating factors before deciding on a sentence:

- A plea of guilty by a company or director is a mitigating factor.
- A previously clean record (ie no previous offences) is a mitigating factor.
- It will be an aggravating feature if the offence has been committed as an ongoing dangerous states of affairs as opposed to being an isolated incident.
- If a company has deliberately breached regulations in order to save money this will be regarded as a seriously aggravating feature.
- The fact that a company is relatively small and does not have specialist safety staff does not act to mitigate what the company has done. The standard of care required by a company is the same whatever its size or financial circumstances.
- A failure to heed warnings is an aggravating feature.
- Steps to remedy deficiencies once drawn to the company's attention act as good mitigation.
- Other factors in environmental cases are likely to include whether the environmental damage caused is 'irreversible' (an aggravating factor) and the level of public concern at what has occurred.
- When considering the seriousness of an offence, previous offences and failure to respond to previous sentences may be taken into account.

The Court of Appeal emphasised that the circumstances of each case vary considerably. The starting point is how far short of the appropriate standard laid down in law, the defendant fell.

Absolute and Conditional Discharges

If the court decides that the circumstances of the offence are such that it is inappropriate to punish the company or director, it may impose an absolute or conditional discharge on an offender.

An absolute discharge is as its name suggests and no punishment follows the event. A conditional discharge is a discharge on the condition that no further offence is committed during the period of the discharge, which will be a maximum of three years. If a further offence is committed, then the offender is liable to be sentenced again for the original offence as well as the new offence.

EXAMPLE

In the case of *CPC (UK)* v *NRA* [1995] Env LR131, CPC owned and operated a factory producing dairy products. Following a pipe fracture, 168 gallons of cleaning liquid escaped through a storm drain into the river. The fracture was caused by a defect in the piping system because two pipes had not been properly joined together. The pipework had been carried out by specialist sub-contractors some nine months before CPC had bought the premises. The company was charged and convicted for offences under s85 of the Water Resources Act 1991. Although there was an order to pay prosecution costs, the company received an absolute discharge on the basis that there was nothing it could have done to prevent the pollution.

Fines

A fine is the usual penalty imposed for environmental offences. Where the trial takes place in the Crown Court there is no limit as to the fine that may be imposed. In the Magistrates' Court the maximum fine will be set by the relevant legislation. As a general guide the maximum penalty is usually £5000. However, many environmental offences are subject to a higher maximum of £20,000 if the offence takes place on industrial premises. Table 8.1 gives a breakdown of the levels of fines for different types of offence.

The fines are fixed by reference to the seriousness of the offence and the offender's means. Each case will be dealt with according to its particular circumstances. In the case of *R* v *Howe & Son* discussed above, an employee of a small company was electrocuted while cleaning the factory. The company was originally fined £48,000. On appeal the fine was reduced to £15,000 on the basis that the company was a small one with limited resources. The court made it clear that the amount of the fine should reflect the financial means of the offender and reduced the fine.

A pollution incident may involve a number of charges relating to separate offences and in theory it is possible for the maximum penalty to be imposed for each separate offence. However, in practice the court will usually take an 'overall view'.

Custodial Sentences

A company cannot go to jail, so a custodial sentence is not an option for corporate environmental crime. It is, however, an option for a convicted director or other officer. The maximum sentence for each offence is fixed by statute: typically in the Magistrates' Court the maximum will be six months, although in some cases the only permissible penalty will be a fine. In the Crown Court, the maximum sentence is usually two years for environmental offences, although in some more serious cases the term is extended to five years.

Table 8.2 lists offences carrying a custodial sentence if a director is found guilty of the offence in the Crown Court.

Table 8.1 *Schedule of Fines for Environmental Offences*

Offence	*Penalty*
Section 23(2) Environmental Protection Act. Certain more serious offences under Part I EPA, eg operating a prescribed process without authorisation or in breach of conditions, breach of enforcement or prohibition notice or failure to comply with clean-up order.	*Magistrates' Court*: fine not exceeding £20,000
	Crown Court: unlimited fine
Section 23(3) Environmental Protection Act. Other offences under Part I EPA, eg failing to give notices, giving false information, obstructing inspectors.	*Magistrates' Court*: fine not exceeding £5000
	Crown Court: unlimited fine
Section 33(8) Environmental Protection Act. Offences of unlawful disposal, etc of controlled waste.	*Magistrates' Court*: fine not exceeding £20,000
	Crown Court: unlimited fine
Section 33(9) Environmental Protection Act. Offences of unlawful disposal, etc involving special waste.	*Magistrates' Court*: fine not exceeding £20,000
	Crown Court: unlimited fine
Section 34(6) Environmental Protection Act. Breach of duty of care relating to waste.	*Magistrates' Court*: fine not exceeding £5000
	Crown Court: unlimited fine

A court will not impose a custodial sentence on an offender unless it is of the opinion that the offence, or the combination of the offence and one other offence associated with it, was so serious that only a custodial sentence can be justified: reasons for the sentence must be explained to the offender. The length of the sentence will be for as long as the court thinks appropriate according to the seriousness of the offence.

Before forming a view on the seriousness of the offence for the purpose of custodial sentencing, the court must obtain and consider a pre-sentence report (submitted by a probation officer or social worker) and must take into account all available information about the circumstances of the offence (including any aggravating or mitigating factors).

EXAMPLE

The owner of a milk bottling business was the first person to be sent to prison for a water pollution offence. A nearby stream and pond were polluted by gas oil which the Agency traced to an unbunded storage tank on premises. He was given a two-month prison sentence (*ENDS Report* 273, October 1997).

Table 8.2 *Custodial Sentences for Environmental Offences*

Integrated Pollution Prevention and Control (IPPC) and Integrated Pollution Control (IPC) offences	
• Operating a prescribed process without an IPC authorisation or in breach of conditions. • Breaching an enforcement or a prohibition notice. • Failing to comply with a clean-up order. • Giving an inspector false information. • Obstructing an inspector.	*Crown Court:* Maximum 2 years imprisonment (5 years for certain IPPC offences) Magistrates' Court: 6 months
Waste offences	
• Unlawful disposal etc of controlled waste.	Crown Court: 2 years Magistrates' Court: 6 months
Special waste offences	
• Offences of unlawful disposal involving special waste.	Crown Court: 5 years Magistrates' Court: 6 months

EXAMPLE

The director of a water company was imprisoned for 18 months for dumping more than 100 tonnes of high-risk clinical waste. 61,000 yellow bags of decomposing clinical waste and drums containing body tissues and amputated limbs were found in a warehouse. The warehouse was supposed to be used for waste paper shredding (*R* v *Hertfordshire County Council, ex parte Green Environmental Industries* [1997] Env LR 329).

EXAMPLE

The operator of a long-standing unlicensed landfill was sentenced to 21 months in prison. Despite repeated warnings from the Environment Agency he continued to accept waste on to the site and ignored an Agency notice requiring him to move the waste. The Agency mounted an 18 month surveillance operation using covert filming (*ENDS Report* 282, July 1998).

EXAMPLE

Two men paid to dispose of 30 drums of waste chemicals, dumped the waste at a former traveller's site and pickaxed the drums to make them drain. The clean-up operation cost £20,000. The men were sentenced to two years in prison. They had earlier run away from court . ENDS described the sentence as the toughest so far for an environmental offence (*ENDS Report* 277, February 1999).

Suspended Sentences

A court may decide to impose a suspended prison sentence. This means that the sentence does not take effect unless the offender commits another offence during a period (called the 'operational period') of between one and two years from the date of the order.

Where the offender commits another offence during the operational period the suspended sentence is activated and the court must deal with it at the same time as sentencing in respect of the fresh offence.

A suspended sentence will often be considered appropriate where the facts of the offence fully justify imprisonment but where the risk of re-offending by the accused is considered to be minimal. It is sometimes seen as a suitable penalty for environmental offences that in themselves are serious, but where the individual has no record of similar past offences and is unlikely to re-offend.

EXAMPLE

The owner of a business that illegally deposited 20,000 tonnes of waste on site was given a four month prison sentence suspended for two years and fined £5000. The court also ordered that his vehicles be confiscated (*ENDS Report* 284, September 1998).

Community Sentences

Another option for a court is a 'community order' against the individual offender. Unlike some jurisdictions, for example, such orders cannot be made against companies in the UK. Such orders include:

- probation;
- community service; and
- supervision.

The criteria for imposing such an order is that the offence, or the combination of the offence and one other offence associated with it, must be serious enough to warrant such a sentence. The order or orders must be suitable for the offender, and any resulting restrictions on liberty imposed by the order must be commensurate with the seriousness of the offence.

EXAMPLE

A director of a Yorkshire drum cleaning company was ordered to do 60 hours of community service after being convicted of five breaches of an IPC authorisation. The court accepted that the director had no assets and that neither a fine nor a custodial sentence was appropriate (*ENDS Report* 281, June 1998).

Prosecution Costs

If a company or director is found guilty of an offence it or he/she may be ordered to pay all or part of the prosecution's costs. In environmental cases these may be significant and may for example include the costs of sampling and analysis: it is not unknown for such costs to exceed the amount of any fine.

EXAMPLE

Anglian Water was fined £15,000 and ordered to pay costs of £2600 after admitting polluting a brook with sludge. The court heard that the incident was due to the failure of the company's monitoring systems (*ENDS Report* 290, March 1999).

EXAMPLE

Esso was fined £13,500 and ordered to pay costs of £300 after a leak from one of its service stations caused thousands of litres of petrol to pollute a drinking water aquifer (*ENDS Report* 289, February 1999).

Compensation Orders

The court may order an offender to pay compensation to any person injured or who suffers loss by the commission of the offence. In theory, this power could be used for environmental or safety offences, but the courts have made it clear that the power should not be used in complex cases where it may be difficult to assess the compensation adequately. This may well preclude its use in many pollution cases.

EXAMPLE

A company director who was fined for assaulting two Health and Safety Executive inspectors was ordered to pay one of the inspectors £200 compensation. The magistrates took a serious view of the offences, particularly as they involved 'public officials carrying out their duties' (*The Safety & Health Practitioner*, August 1999).

Disqualification

By section 2 of the Company Directors Disqualification Act 1986, a court may make a disqualification order against a person where he is convicted of an indictable offence whether in the Crown Court or Magistrates' Court. Most environmental offences are indictable in the sense that they are triable 'either way' (ie in both types of court). The effect is to prohibit the individual, without the leave of the court, from:

- being a director of a company;
- being a receiver or manager of a company's properties; or
- being concerned or taking part in the promotion, formation or management of a company in any way, directly or indirectly.

The maximum period of disqualification in the Magistrates' Court is 5 years, and in the Crown Court 15 years.

Disqualification is not an idle threat and is being used as a stick to force directors to attain higher standards. The Government has stressed in Parliament that disqualification is intended to apply equally to safety legislation as to offences concerned with the financial mismanagement of companies.

EXAMPLE

'Director disqualified after conviction for safety offence'

A company director has been disqualified from being a director for two years following conviction for a safety offence. This was in addition to a fine of £5000 imposed on the director personally.

The director ignored a prohibition notice served by the HSE over unsafe working practices in a quarry. The director was prosecuted on the basis he knew of the dangers in the quarry but still placed men in great danger and deliberately continued to extract minerals without a safe system of work (*HS Monitor*, Vol 15, Issue 8, August 1992).

'Relevant Offences'

There is one final (and potentially very serious) consequence of the conviction of a company director. Environmental legislation imposes in certain cases the ability to discriminate against a company in granting licences, where the company or a 'relevant person' (which will include directors, managers, employees and business partners) has been convicted of a prescribed range of offences.

Examples include:

- The test of 'fit and proper person' relating to the grant and revocation of waste management licences under Part II of the Environmental Protection Act 1990.
- The registration of waste carriers under the Control of Pollution (Amendment) Act 1989.

Thus, the conviction of a director for certain offences could jeopardise his company's ability to function, which is a serious threat. Furthermore, if a director moves companies, his conviction may follow him and affect his new company. Conviction could therefore in effect make a Director unemployable in certain sectors (at least until the conviction is spent).

EXAMPLE

The director of Lions & Tigers Ltd was convicted, along with the company, of depositing waste in contravention of the company's waste management licence. The following year the company expanded its operations and bought a second site. The Environment Agency rejected its application for a waste management licence in light of the conviction.

There may be other consequences:

EXAMPLE

A registered waste carrier was prosecuted successfully for failing to disclose when he applied for registration that he had a previous conviction for an environmental offence (*ENDS Report* 222, July 1993).

CHAPTER 9
CIVIL LIABILITY

Attention quite naturally tends to focus on the potential criminal liability of directors. However, the potential for civil liability should be equally worrying. Criminal fines can be small change compared with the enormous civil damages, clean-up costs and legal costs that can result from a pollution incident.

It is more usual for a victim of environmental damage to bring a civil claim against a company than a director. It is easier to proceed against the company and a company is more likely to have enough money to satisfy any judgment by the court. There are, however, situations in which a director can be made personally liable. If a director has himself behaved negligently, he can sometimes be held personally liable.

EXAMPLE

Director Brenda, while walking through the site on her way home, spots a valve that she thinks has been left open. She 'closes' it but in fact, she has negligently, opened it. Overnight a neighbouring trout farm is decimated by the escaping effluent. Brenda could be personally liable, as well as her company, if the owners of the trout farm bring an action for the loss of the fish.

The acts of Brenda are more likely to be attributed to the company unless she has led someone to believe that she has taken a special responsibility for the person who suffers loss by her actions, over and above the company, in which case she can be held personally liable.

EXAMPLE

Director Peter tells the owner of a neighbouring salmon farm not to worry about his company's activities. He tells him not to bother writing officially to the company to enquire about contamination levels in a local water course. He can personally reassure him that the levels are safe. Peter will be personally liable if the levels kill the fish.

A director can also be personally liable, jointly with the company, even if acts causing the wrong have been caused by other employees of the company by virtue of their being the controlling will or mind of the company. The courts, however, have recognised that it may be undesirable to make a director personally liable in too many situations as this could act as a disincentive to enterprise and encourage actions against directors' for tactical purposes in order to put pressure on the company to settle a legal action.

> *EXAMPLE*
>
> Rockoil Ltd is a major oil company operating a large depot in an urban area. Local residents complain of smuts and fumes that cause damage to property and make them feel ill. The residents get legal aid for an action in nuisance against Rockoil Ltd. Subsequently, three local residents who claim to have contracted cancer from emissions obtain legal aid for actions in nuisance, negligence and under the legal principle named after the case which established it, '*Rylands* v *Fletcher*'. Writs are also issued against the entire board of directors of Rockoil Ltd, who it is said should have been aware for many years of the environmental problems the depot was causing. In the absence of any direct and personal involvement by the directors with the pollution problems, it is probably unlikely that the personal actions would succeed – an application might be made to strike them out. The court may well see the actions as an attempt to obtain publicity and to embarrass the company.

The court in *C Evans & Sons Ltd* v *Spritebrand Ltd* [1958] 2 All ER 415 indicated that:

- suing a director as well as the company for tactical purposes, to exert pressure to settle, should be discouraged;
- the personal liability of the director cannot be greater than that of the company, so any knowledge or intention required on the part of the company will also be required on the part of the director;
- a director should not be treated more kindly than the servant who committed the tort when taking his orders from the director; and
- broad policy considerations can be material to deciding whether or not the director is liable.

If, however, the director has authorised the acts that have caused the wrong or played a more personal part in the acts complained of, he may be made personally liable.

> *'A tort may be committed through an officer or servant of a company without the chairman or managing director being in any way implicated. There are many such cases reported in the books. If, however, the chairman or managing director procures or directs the commission of the tort he may be personally liable for the tort and the damage flowing from it . . . each case depends on its own particular facts.'* (Lord Salmon in *Wah Tat Bank Ltd* v *Chan Cheng Kum* [1975] 2 All ER 257.

> *EXAMPLE*
>
> Arthur, the managing director of a small printing company, tells an employee to put some carboys of waste acid into the bottom of a skip that is ready for collection and cover it with waste paper. The skip is collected and when it is deposited at the landfill site, the site operator is blinded when one of the carboys breaks. Arthur could be personally liable to the operator.

If a company is sued, it may decide to take action against a director it considers has acted negligently:

- It could claim a contribution from the director under s1 Civil Liability (Contribution) Act 1987 if the director is also personally liable for the damage caused.
- It could sue the director for breach of his service contract or breach of his duty of care.

Injunctions

Civil proceedings may result in an injunction being granted against a company. An injunction may regulate the hours when a company can carry out its operations or it may require the factory to be closed down completely. Alternatively, a company may give an undertaking to a court promising to refrain from certain acts or to comply with certain requirements.

> *EXAMPLE*
>
> Zanzibar plc is carrying out a process that causes a lot of noise and fumes. The local council receives a large number of complaints. It decides to ask the court for an injunction. The company agrees to give an undertaking (ie a 'promise') to the court to carry out certain remedial works to lessen the noise and fumes.

What happens to a director where an injunction is breached or an undertaking not complied with? Breach of an undertaking or an injunction is a contempt of court and can lead to an order committing the person responsible to prison.

An order committing an officer of a company to prison can only be made if that person has been responsible for the company's breach of the court's orders. A director who is aware of the terms of the court order is under a duty to take reasonable care to secure the company's compliance with it. If he fails in this duty he will be punished for contempt of court notwithstanding that he had not actively participated in the breach. However, a director who was aware of the order but remained passive and did nothing to interfere with the administration of justice and did not wilfully ignore the breaches of the order would not be liable for committal simply on the basis that he was a director of the company.

> *EXAMPLE*
>
> In a 1990 case (*Attorney General* v *Tuvalu Philatelic Distribution Corporation Limited* [1990] 1 WLR 926) the chairman and managing director of a number of companies was found to be in contempt of court on the basis that he had knowingly caused or permitted breaches of court orders and undertakings obtained against his company. He was sentenced to three months' imprisonment with a fine of £3000. He appealed and the prison sentence was quashed as being too severe for a married man of 49 with a family and a previously good record and character.

CHAPTER 10
WHISTLEBLOWING

Any evidence before a court about the shortcomings in the environmental performance of a company may well be provided by an employee concerned about damage being done to the environment. A director may himself have concerns but find himself prevented from speaking out by the other directors. The colloquial term for speaking out is 'whistleblowing'. It refers to the disclosure by an employee (or professional) of confidential information relating to some danger or other illegal conduct. Whistleblowing is an option of last resort but it may become more common as environmental sensibilities among employees increases.

The increasing interest in the subject of whistleblowing can be explained by a number of factors including recent health and safety disasters such as the *Herald of Free Enterprise* ferry tragedy, where 193 people died because the bow doors on the ship were left open. Concerns had been expressed on at least five occasions about the safety of ferries sailing with their bow doors open, but employee's concerns were either ignored or got 'lost' in middle management.

> *EXAMPLE*
>
> The director of a Suffolk chemical company discovered that a number of leaking drums had been buried under the company site. His fellow directors would not let him inform the regulatory authority that the company had buried several hundred drums of waste just above an aquifer. He found himself dismissed and had to fight for three years to obtain compensation from the company – with consequent stress and financial hardship in the process (*ENDS Report*, October 1997).

Workers who blow the whistle by disclosing information about certain types of matters are now protected under the Public Interest Disclosure Act 1998 from being dismissed or penalised by their employers as a result.

Workers

A 'worker' is defined widely to include those under traditional contracts of employment, but also those supplied by third parties and even those on work experience.

If a worker discloses information that reveals:

- that a company is committing, or about to commit, a criminal offence; or
- its activities are damaging the environment; or
- endangering the health and safety of any individual;

he has the right not to be subjected to any detrimental treatment by his employer because he has disclosed the information. In particular, if he is dismissed because of the disclosure then this will amount to an unfair dismissal. An employee who feels that they have been subjected to any detriment can complain to an employment tribunal.

Good Faith

Any disclosure of information must not be made maliciously or frivolously. To prevent this occurring, an employee will only be entitled to protection if he/she makes the disclosure in 'good faith' and in the 'reasonable belief' that it reveals environmental or health and safety wrongdoing.

Disclosure to Whom?

Anyone concerned about a company's activities should first talk to senior management. If a director has concerns he should approach the other directors. Disclosure of any information could also be to a lawyer.

Although an employee is expected to raise the issues within the companythey will also be protected if they 'go public' with the information (including to the media) providing that they reasonably believe that their employer will victimise them if told about the concerns or if they have already told their employer.

The employee must act in good faith, must reasonably believe that the information disclosed is substantially true, that it is not made for personal gain and that it is a reasonable step for them to take. If the information discloses an exceptionally serious failure in the company, an employee can go public without having to talk to the company first providing they do so in good faith.

Avoiding Whistleblowing

It is important to let employees report any concerns that they might have about the company's operations and to encourage, as far as possible, the view that whistleblowers are not troublemakers but dedicated individuals who provide a valuable early warning system.

Companies may wish to set up 'a whistleblowing procedure' that might include:

- a clear statement that malpractice is taken seriously in the organisation and an indication of the sorts of matters regarded as malpractice (for example, breaches of environmental legislation);
- respect for the confidentiality of staff raising concerns if they wish and the opportunity to raise concerns outside the line management structure;
- disciplinary procedures for making false and malicious allegations;
- an indication of the proper way in which concerns may be raised outside the organisation if necessary;
- a list of specific people who can be approached and who are known to be sympathetic and personable; and
- a telephone 'hotline' or direct access to the chief executive.

CHAPTER 11
INSURANCE AND INDEMNITY

Many directors may feel that their exposure to legal liability is limited in practice either by an insurance or by the likelihood that their company will 'see them all right' and indemnify them against any liability. However, such a belief could turn out to be seriously misconceived.

First of all as a matter of public policy it is impossible to insure against criminal penalties or the consequences of conviction. The same is true of any agreement that one party shall indemnify another against such consequences. The general principle was stated in one case where it was said:

> *'A law which imposes a punishment as distinguished from a payment of compensation is defeated by the punishment being passed on to another'* (*Leslie* v *Reliable Advertising Agency* [1915] 1 KB 652 at p659).

The reason for this rule is that in criminal courts the punishment is fixed with regard to the personal responsibility of the offender, to deter and to affect that offender's future conduct. These objectives would be defeated if the offender were able to recover the amount of the fine from someone else.

However, there is nothing to stop a company paying someone's fine voluntarily; the rule simply renders unenforceable any agreement to do so. In Canada, the court in the *Bata* case went so far as to impose an order that the company should in no circumstances pay the director's fines (see Appendix I). Such an order would probably not be possible in the English courts as penalties available to the courts are laid down by statute, which do not specify this course as being available.

It is possible for a company to agree to indemnify a director against *civil* liability and against the legal costs of defending criminal or civil proceedings (see below). What remains to be tested is whether statutory clean-up costs (which may in some cases only be awarded where an offence has been committed) are categorised as criminal penalties for the purposes of the public policy rule prohibiting indemnities for criminal convictions.

Under the 1989 Companies Act a company can itself indemnify a director or purchase an insurance policy for its directors to indemnify them against certain types of liability including any liability incurred in defending any proceedings (whether civil or criminal) in which judgment is given in the directors favour or they are acquitted. This is known as a 'directors and officers' ('D & O') liability policy.

Such a policy will cover all of the directors and officers of a company providing full protection with relatively high limits of indemnity. As well as indemnifying the individual director or officer, the policy will also indemnify the company in those circumstances in which it is allowed to reimburse the director for legal costs or compensation payments ordered against them. The policy is written on a 'claims made' basis irrespective of when the alleged wrongful act took place. A director may also take out, at his own expense, personal insurance to cover the cost of a criminal prosecution, but not the penalty imposed on the guilty offender.

Directors and officers' insurance is, however, likely to be unhelpful in respect of environmental liability because the policies generally exclude liability for pollution and clean-up costs. (This is the case for most public-liability insurance policies currently available on the market.)

However, the terms of such exclusions vary considerably and it is important to analyse the actual wording of the exclusion. Consideration should be given as to whether or not the exclusion is restricted to civil claims, or whether it extends also to include criminal prosecutions. The exclusion may be limited to gradual pollution though it may also cover 'sudden and accidental' events.

Most directors and officers policies exclude employees from the coverage so in most cases it is relatively easy to determine whether or not a person is a director or officer of the company as there will be a formal appointment. However, it may be unclear whether a particular person employed by the company is a director or officer or simply an employee or some form of independent contractor. There is no definitive answer to this in the legislation. A further area of difficulty concerns persons who have not been formally appointed by the company but who have acted on its behalf for many years. Again it is unclear whether they are within the scope of insurance. The same applies for shadow directors.

CHAPTER 12
SOME PRACTICAL ADVICE

Set out below are a number of practical points, some of which are self-explanatory, on limiting exposure to environmental liability.

1 *It is important to know why environmental problems occur and to take preventative measures*

> *EXAMPLE*
>
> PharmaCorp ensures that all of its chemical storage tanks are properly bunded to appropriate standards, whereas MediComp does not bund any of their tanks. Should, for example, a forklift truck damage one of the tanks at either of the premises, PharmaCorp would not cause any pollution whereas MediComp may lose the contents of the tank to either the ground or possibly into surface waters. Thus, MediComp runs the risk of incurring liability in relation to the released chemical.

Vandalism is an increasing worry: particularly as the House of Lords has made it clear that companies are expected to guard against the acts of vandals and will be liable for any pollution caused by their activities. Companies will need to have in place adequate security measures to guard against vandalism or other malicious conduct.

In *Empress Car Company (Abertillery) Ltd* v *National Rivers Authority* ([1998] Env LR 385) the company stored oil in a tank, the tap of which was connected to a hose. Vandals opened the tap (which was not locked) leading to an escape of oil into the river. Had the company caused this pollution?

The House of Lords distinguished between ordinary 'facts of life' that companies could be expected to guard against, and wholly unexpected events, which they were not. 'Ordinary' vandalism is, regrettably, a fact of life and the company remained liable for the pollution. On the other hand, a terrorist attack would not have been regarded as an 'ordinary fact of life' at this site.

In another case heard shortly before the *Empress Car Company* decision, it was held that the bursting of a seal on pipework was an 'ordinary fact of life', whether or not it was actually foreseeable. The company in question was liable for the pollution caused by the failure (*Environment Agency* v *Brock plc* [1998] Env LR 607).

2 *Training of staff*

It is good management to ensure that all staff are knowledgeable and prepared for an accident or incident at the company. It is important to make employees aware that it is risky for them to talk to regulators or third parties in an uncontrolled manner. This is particularly the case if litigation is in progress or underway. A regulator's decision to prosecute or take more tough action may be made on the basis of casual comments by staff that reveal issues the regulator had not previously been aware of. It may be useful to provide employees with training on the powers and rights that they have when being questioned by regulatory authorities (see Chapter 6).

EXAMPLE

Oikas UK, and one of its directors, have been prosecuted by the local authority for noise pollution offences. In discussion outside court, it becomes clear that the authority is taking a tough line as a result of 'information' it has picked up during 'chats' with staff during site visits.

3 *Human error*

Human error is the cause of many pollution incidents and problems. As discussed in Chapter 2, most environmental offences are of a strict liability nature and thus the fact that there was no intention to pollute on the part of the offender is not relevant as to whether or not a criminal offence has been committed.

EXAMPLE

Company employee, Bob, was delivering heating fuel oil to one of the company's office premises. Bob misread his delivery docket and delivered 8000 litres of oil into a tank only capable of holding 1800 litres. The fuel oil overflowed the tank and its bunding and then entered the adjacent canal. There was no intention on the part of the employee to pollute the canal, but nevertheless, the company was held responsible. If the problem had been anticipated in the first instance, the tank would have been fitted with alarms or other safety devices to ensure it was not overfilled.

4 *Allocating money and time resources to sorting out problems*

The courts have made it clear that a company's financial problems are no excuse for evading environmental obligations. Damaging the environment has been made a crime to demonstrate the seriousness with which they are regarded. It is also clear that a company must put aside money to carry out any investment necessary as a result of changes in environmental laws.

EXAMPLES

In the Bata case (discussed in further detail in Appendix I), Mr Keith Weston was found guilty under the Environmental Protection Act (Canada). A lesson that came out of the case was that Mr Weston was not entitled to rely on delegation unless (a) the delegate was properly trained, and (b) the delegates had all of the resources to do the job. A company's financial difficulties were felt to be no excuse in this regard.

5 *Recording decisions and dissent to decisions*

It is important to keep a documentary record of any important decisions made with respect to environmental practices, particularly if the decisions appear to be dubious or based only on consideration of profits.

> *EXAMPLE*
>
> Wastetickets plc recently commissioned a compliance audit for discharges in to the local river. The company felt compelled to undertake monitoring after pressure from the Environment Agency. The results of the monitoring revealed a significant amount of pollution entering the river from the site. The subsequent board meeting decided to ignore the problem unless their hand was forced. However, Mr Davis, a fairly junior member on the board dissented and insisted his opinion was recorded in the meeting's minutes. The Environment Agency brought prosecutions against the company for 'causing' the pollution and against the individual board members for 'knowingly permitting' the pollution. Mr Davis was able to convince the Agency to drop the prosecution against him on the basis that, although a board member, he had dissented from the decision and had a documentary record of that dissent. Mr Davis had not been in a position to prevent the pollution and thus could not have knowingly permitted it.

6 *Preserve evidence*

However, retaining documents can carry its own risks. In civil litigation there is an obligation to list and reveal all documentation relevant to proceedings during a process known as discovery. Those documents that do not have to be revealed to the other party are known as privileged documents. (This is a complex subject and if the need arises, legal advice should be obtained.)

An environmental report will not be privileged and will have to be produced to an opponent in litigation. However, there may be ways of attempting to fix such a report with the necessary privilege to prevent its production in litigation and, when commissioning an environmental audit, it may be worth considering this further.

> *EXAMPLE*
>
> SlyCo discovered an oil leak that had been contaminating a local well for some time. The company immediately destroyed all documents relating to the problem. When a neighbour brought a civil action against SlyCo in relation to the polluted drinking water, the court made adverse assumptions about the missing documentation.

7 *Disclosure of confidential information*

It can be a painful surprise to a company to find that when it becomes involved in legal disputes or investigation by statutory authorities, documents that it has disclosed to a regulatory authority but regards as highly confidential and privileged are in the public domain.

It is important to realise that the Environment Agency is under an obligation to disclose much information it holds in response to any request for the information. There are exceptions to this obligation where information should be treated as confidential. Information supplied voluntarily to the Agency may be exempt from publication as is information that forms the subject matter of a potential inquiry by the Agency. The Agency has its own information policy which states that the Agency will not allow the public access to information that is business information or confidential information of a sensitive nature.

It is important to be aware of the risks of publication and of the potential exemptions from publication when a company supplies information to the Agency. The Agency should be told of the confidential nature of the information and it should be made clear that the company presumes that the information will remain confidential.

8 *Co-operation with regulators and emergency services*

As discussed in Chapter 6, there is a fine balancing act to be achieved between protecting the interests of a company following an incident and co-operating with the emergency services and regulators in order to ensure that any problems are dealt with efficiently and safely.

> *EXAMPLE*
>
> Shell UK Limited was prosecuted for pollution of the Mersey in 1990 when 156 tonnes of crude oil leaked into the Mersey from a corroded section of Shell's pipeline. It was revealed that the company had not informed the National Rivers Authority promptly and had not complied with the advice of the National Rivers Authority on how to deal with the spill. The judge took a dim view of this behaviour and the £1 million fine reflected his opinion (*ENDS Report* 181, February 1995).

9 *The use of an environmental management system (EMS)*

Companies should certainly consider implementing an environmental management system (EMS) that should lessen the chances of unexpected environmental problems arising. In the event of anything going wrong, regulators are likely to take into account the fact that a company has an EMS when deciding whether or not to prosecute and view favourably the existence of an EMS.

The British Standards Institution has developed an EMS known as BS7750. A company wishing to be registered under the standard must set up and maintain a documented system to ensure that it meets its environmental policies and objectives and is able to demonstrate its compliance to third parties. Under BS7750 the company would be expected to:

(i) carry out a preparatory environmental review of its activities;

(ii) draw up an environmental policy stating its policy and objectives, responsibilities within its organisation and a programme for achieving its objectives;

(iii) draw up a manual documenting the above, as well as setting up a system of keeping records to provide an audit trail; and

(iv) arrange regular audits to determine that the system is working according to specification and that it is effective and meeting the company's environmental policies and objectives.

The audit is an important tool in any EMS. If the body verifying the EMS has a good opinion of the way in which a company carries out its audit and the competence of the auditors, it is less likely to intervene as much in the company's operations, which will in turn reduce costs.

The European Commission set up an Eco-Audit Scheme in 1992. The scheme is very similar to the BS7750 Scheme and requires the company to initiate an EMS. Clearly, registering under BS7750 should reduce the steps a company would need to make to comply with the requirements of the Eco-Audit regulation.

The scheme has, however, not performed very well and there has been a low take-up rate. This seems to have been due to various factors such as the existence of national schemes and the cumbersome procedures involved in establishing the scheme within a company. In response the Commission has revised the scheme and it remains to be seen whether its popularity increases.

An international standard for environmental management systems has also been developed. The International Standards Organisation (ISO) 14000 series provides a framework of organisational and product standards for managing environmental issues and impacts.

The ISO 14000 series builds directly on BS7750 (which was the world's first such standard) and reflects many features of the Commission scheme.

ISO 14001 is the foundation stone for the series. It defines five elements:

(i) An environmental policy

(ii) An assessment of a business's environmental aspects

(iii) A management system

(iv) A series of internal audits and reports to senior management

(v) A public declaration that the system is being implemented.

ISO 14001 is widely viewed as being more suited than EMAS to the needs of large organisation with operations outside of Europe.

10 *Be aware of the risks and benefits of compliance audits*

One of the chief objectives of environmental audits is to avoid litigation or other claims. It is, however, important to be aware that, paradoxically, these studies may increase the exposure to such a claim.

EXAMPLE

Assembla Inc undertakes an environmental audit of its processes. The audit reveals an imminent risk to health and safety from a heating plant on the factory floor. However, Assembla Inc is not in a financial position to remedy the position. At a later date, three of the valves at the plant burst and two employees are burnt by steam. In subsequent litigation, the environmental report is revealed and proves useful evidence for the plaintiffs in establishing the company's awareness of the problem.

Clearly, Assembla Inc was placed in an awkward position. Only by revealing latent defects can the company remedy them. In doing so the company may be fixed with knowledge and consequently liable for something that it cannot immediately put right.

Should a situation like this arise, the company should state clearly in writing, the reasons why the problems cannot immediately be addressed, together with a definite schedule for ensuring that the matters are dealt with either on an emergency basis or in due course on a timely basis.

11 *Anticipate what may happen*

One of the benefits of having undertaken thorough environmental audits and reviews and having put appropriate procedures in place at a plant is that the potential problems arising from an incident at a factory can be anticipated and be prevented or mitigated. A situation can be made far worse by inadequate handling.

A company with proper procedures in place prior to an incident can deal with an incident in accordance with those procedures in a prudent manner, and will have much better standing with environmental regulators and any court, should proceedings ensue.

EXAMPLE

Allied Colloids were prosecuted over a huge blaze in Bradford in July 1992. The fire caused damage estimated at approximately £6 million. There were 36 fire engines in attendance, and a large amount of fire fighting water escaped into the River Calder along with washed-away toxic chemicals. In the event, local residents were evacuated and 34 people received medical treatment. The fire arose from serious malpractice in chemical storage procedures; a readily combustible chemical was badly stored. It was stored in an inappropriate manner next to a strong oxidising agent. Additionally, fire-fighting was hampered by a lack of water as the company's dam had dried up in 1988. The company was fined £40,000 and additionally had to pay costs of £62,300. The Judge commented that 'it was a serious breach of duty' that Allied Colloids had not made the implementation of the Health and Safety Executive guidelines the responsibility of a qualified chemical engineer (*ENDS Report* 211, August 1992)

CHAPTER 13
MANAGING A CRISIS

Set out below are some brief practical comments on how to deal with and be prepared for an accident or emergency.

Preparation Checklist

1 Establish good communications within the company.

2 Foster sound health and safety practices (full compliance with relevant health and safety legislation).

3 Foster good environmental policies within the company (full compliance with environmental legislation).

4 Establish a 'whistleblowing' procedure to enable employees to raise any concerns.

5 Obtain the services of respected crisis management consultants.

6 Enlist their services to carry out a crisis management audit.

7 Set up and train a crisis management team within the company.

8 Carry out regular authentic simulations.

9 Prepare a manual of crisis response plans.

10 Set up procedures and checklists for the crisis management team.

11 Check all insurance policies for their relevance and validity in the light of the crisis management audit.

12 Obtain the views of insurers on the crisis response plan.

13 Retain lawyers to discuss their role and plan of action in the event of a crisis.

14 Obtain the views of insurers on the allocated role of the company's lawyers.

15 Establish and maintain good relations/communication with the press/media.

Incident Checklist

1 Evacuate the premises (if appropriate).

2 Notify the emergency services and the police.

3 Notify the HSE, the Environment Agency, the local authority and/or any other appropriate bodies.

4 Arrange for unhindered access to the site (if appropriate).

5 Where firemen are involved, take appropriate steps to maintain the company's duty of care for them.

6 Telephone and write to the company's underwriters' claims department.

7 Ensure close liaison between the crisis management team and the insurer's representative.

8 Use a single spokesman from the crisis management team.

9 Keep press interviews to a minimum.

10 Obtain clearance from the company's lawyers regarding any press releases, particularly the initial press release.

11 Ensure that the reports relating to the incident are prepared by the company's lawyers.

12 Mark all of memoranda 'prepared for the purposes of litigation'.

13 Arrange for lawyers to keep all relevant documents.

14 Ensure that damaged machinery, etc is clearly labelled and preserved.

15 Take photographs of any damage.

16 Using lawyer's views, decide on the need for an internal inquiry.

17 Take advice from lawyers relating to claims reporting and claims handling procedures to ensure recovery of claims from insurers as soon as possible.

18 Keep in close liaison with insurers and lawyers in relation to the company's attitude to, and immediate settlement of, claims.

19 Provide the regulatory authority investigating the incident with all the help and information it requires, while attempting not to damage the company's position regarding any prosecution. If necessary check with lawyers.

20 Take advice from lawyers on admissions by the company and its directors.

21 Take advice from lawyers on the need to identify expert consultants and witnesses.

22 Sanction company engineers and an independent expert (appointed by the company) to investigate all circumstances of the incident and to preserve evidence.

23 Arrange for witness statements to be taken quickly while memories are still fresh and the witnesses are not swayed by the media coverage.

24 Take advice from lawyers on the plea to be made by the company.

25 Obtain an assessment from the company's engineers and the expert witness, in association with the company's lawyers, on which laws may have been breached.

26 Discuss with lawyers the possible form of criminal prosecutions and civil actions and address possible defences.

27 Consider with lawyers tactics to counter larger claims and collective actions by plaintiffs.

APPENDIX 1
A CANADIAN CASE STUDY – THE BATA INDUSTRIES CASE

Introduction

While most of this report has been concerned with the law of England and Wales, it is sometimes illuminating to look at cases from other jurisdictions. This is particularly true in environmental law, where circumstances in different countries often have a striking and uncanny similarity.

The prosecution of various directors of the giant footwear company, Bata Industries, by the Environmental Protection Agency of Ontario is an extremely instructive case. Although the detailed law is different, many of the points of general principle are exactly the same as in the UK. The case provides a stark warning to directors of the very real risks when things go wrong environmentally, and considers the responsibility of officers at various levels.

The Facts

Bata Industries Limited (BIL) is the Canadian operating company of the Bata Shoe Organisation (BSO), an organisation of various Bata Companies throughout the world. In the late 1980s one of BIL's four divisions, Bata Footwear, operated a footwear manufacturing plant in Batawa, North of Trenton, Ontario.

In the late 1970s and early 1980s, BIL started to produce more shoes and boots that required the introduction of chemical additives and the use of certain cleaning solvents. As a result, a 5000 gallons storage tank of liquid waste was installed. During the 1980s it became difficult to dispose of liquid wastes and as a result drums of waste accumulated at the plant awaiting removal. Between 1986 and 1988 BIL sought and obtained quotes for the removal of the drums. This was a lengthy process as samples were lost and re-analysis was sometimes necessary. An initial quote of $56,000 in 1986 was rejected as being too high; at the time Canada's shoe industry had been decimated by imports and BIL was losing money. A subsequent quote of $28,000 seemed too low and BIL was concerned that the haulier would not dispose of the waste in accordance with the law.

Late in 1988, Keith Weston (a director of the company and the plant manager) left BIL for an assignment to another BSO company in Malaysia. He set aside a reserve of $100,000 to deal with removal of the waste.

The Charges

BIL was charged with unlawfully discharging hazardous waste, contrary to Section 14 Environmental Protection Act 1986 (EPA) and section 30 Ontario Water Resources Act (OWRA). Other charges related to the unlawful operation of a waste management system, the storage of hazardous waste for more than three months without notifying the Ministry of Environment and failing to report the discharge of hazardous waste into the environment and groundwater.

The Ministry of Environment also charged Thomas G Bata Jnr (chairman of the board and a director), Douglas Marchant (president and director) and Keith Weston (the former plant manager and director) with failing to take all reasonable care to prevent unlawful discharges contrary to the EPA and OWRA.

The prosecutions were undoubtedly strategic and selective; the legislation entitled every officer and director to be charged and charges were not filed against (for example) the previous director and president of BIL, the company's property manager, or the vice president responsible for the company before Mr Weston.

Other Interesting Facts

1 Investigations began following a false complaint from an employee that BIL was pouring chemicals into the sanitary sewer system.

2 Ministry of Environment enforcement officers obtained initial information by trespassing on site and by taking photographs that were not revealed to the company. The trial judge ruled that this evidence was not to be excluded as 'fruit of the poisoned tree' as it would not affect the fairness of the trial, did not represent a serious violation of the rights of the accused and would not bring the administration of justice into disrepute. In particular, the drum storage site was in plain view and was well known to the community and BIL was the type of company who would have co-operated with the Ministry of Environment and would not have insisted on a formal search warrant anyway.

3 Douglas Marchant was interviewed in his office in Toronto voluntarily. He was cautioned by Ministry of Environment investigators that he need not give a statement but, if he did, anything which he provided would be used against him. The investigator then read him section 167 EPA which suggested that if he did not provide information he could be charged with obstruction of justice. The statement was ruled inadmissible on the basis that the investigators had effectively compelled Mr Marchant to give a statement, which otherwise he had the legal right not to give if he so chose.

4 The defence disclosed half of their evidence in advance to the Crown, including a copy of the Company's Environmental Policy for handling waste, which had received the input and approval of Thomas G Bata Jnr and Douglas Marchant. Rather than considering whether this policy met the required standard of due diligence, the Ministry of Environment had the document forensically tested to determine when it had been created!

The Findings

The Company was fined $60,000 and received a detailed prohibition order requiring, among other things, $60,000 payments for a local household hazardous waste project, publication of the conviction in the Group's worldwide newsletter, a caution placed on the company register, publication of an advisory circular worldwide and environmental issues to be mandatory on the agenda of all board meetings during the term of the order. Additionally, the company was disallowed from indemnifying the directors for the fine imposed against them as set out below:

Thomas G Bata Jnr – It was concluded that Mr Bata was aware of his environmental responsibilities and had personally approved written directions relating to environmental matters: 'Mr Bata did not allow himself to be wilfully blind to problems or to be orchestrated in his movements when at the plant'. Mr Bata responded to matters that were brought to his attention promptly and appropriately and had placed an experienced director on site: 'Mr Bata was entitled to assume that Mr Weston was addressing environmental concerns at the facility and Mr Bata was entitled to rely upon the system in place, unless he became aware the system was defective.' Mr Bata was held to have met the heavy burden of proving due diligence on his part and was found not guilty.

Douglas Marchant – The judge held that Mr Marchant was required to exercise the highest degree of supervision and control, one that demonstrated that he was exhorting those whom he might normally be expected to influence or control to an accepted standard or behaviour. His responsibilities were not only to give instructions, but also to see to it that they were carried out. Mr Marchant had assisted with issuing the company's environmental policy, but had not done all that was required of him personally to ensure it was properly implemented. Unlike Mr Bata, Mr Marchant was not entitled to rely on Mr Weston. There was some evidence of activity on his part to direct removal of the waste when the matter was brought to his attention, but the level of activity was not enough. Mr Marchant was convicted and fined $12,000.

Keith Weston – Mr Weston, as the on-site manager, had the highest degree of responsibility of the three personal defendants although, significantly, he travelled extensively throughout Canada in a marketing role. He delegated the responsibility of environmental matters to his subordinate, and was held by the judge not to have given the subordinate the financial resources to take up and implement decisions on his own. In taking on his job, Mr Weston had demanded and received complete authority to manage the plant and, having received the authority, he was not entitled to rely on delegation unless (a) the delegate was properly trained and (b) the delegate had all the resources to do the job. The company's financial difficulties were no excuse in this respect. Mr Weston was convicted and fined $12,000.

The Appeal

BIL, Mr Marchant and Mr Weston all appealed against their sentences. The appeal judge felt that the trial judge had not given sufficient credit to the company for the amount of community and environmental action it had undertaken. The $60,000 required for starting up the local household waste programme was reduced to $30,000 on that basis.

In the same vein, it was held that the $12,000 fines for each of the individuals were too high and they were halved to $6000.

In relation to the company probation order; the distribution of any newsletter outlining the facts of the case was to be confined to provinces in Canada. Additionally, no obligation could be imposed on group companies other than Bata. The rest of the probation order remained substantially unchanged.

Lessons to Be Learnt from Bata?

1 *Responsibility*

The board of directors is ultimately responsible for environmental compliance.

2 *Delegation*

If the board chooses to delegate, it must ensure that the system is adequately and effectively supervised with delegates being properly educated and having adequate resources.

3 *Reliance*

The board is entitled to place reasonable reliance upon delegates and on reports provided to the board.

4 *Policy*

There should be a corporate environmental policy approved by the board dealing with the prevention of pollution. The board should regularly ensure that the policy is being complied with. This may involve (in most cases would necessarily involve) the conducting of environmental audits.

5 *Standards*

The board should be aware of the standards in their own industry, as well as other industries that may deal with similar environmental concerns, such as waste.

6 *Records*

In Canadian Law (the position in the UK may well be different) the onus is on directors to prove they were duly diligent. The court will wish to see relevant minutes of board meetings reflecting adequate considerations of environmental matters.

7 *Action*

The board should, as soon as possible, be informed of, and react to, environmental concerns that affect the company.